To Teach A Child

Ida Nelle Hollaway

BROADMAN PRESS
Nashville, Tennessee

© Copyright 1979
Broadman Press.

All rights reserved.

4256-34
ISBN: 0-8054-5634-1

Dewey Decimal Classification: 301.42
Subject heading: FAMILY // PARENT
AND CHILD

Library of Congress Catalog Card
Number: 78-74094
Printed in the United States of
America.

Preface

This book is written from several stances: as a mother, as a public school teacher, as a worker with young children in Sunday School, and as a responsible citizen in a country I cherish. No matter which of these the reader has in common with me, it is my sincere hope that my message comes through loud and clear: *Our children need us, all of us, in all circumstances.*

The names of people in the examples used in this book all have been changed. In some cases, the examples are really composite pictures of people with a common problem or who have dramatized a situation for me.

I owe sincere thanks to Dr. William Penrod, professor of psychology at Middle Tennessee State University and head of the Institute of Christian Ministries in Nashville, Tennessee, for his time and patient effort in checking the soundness of the interpretations given here.

I also owe much appreciation to my husband, Ernest, for his continuing encouragement and help.

To our own children,
Lee, Bill, Stephen, Mark, and Becca,
who have taught us at least as much
as we have taught them,
and
To our grandchildren,
who make the whole process wonderfully worthwhile.

Contents

1. It Takes All of Us 7
2. It's Me, Mom! 18
3. The Greatest of These 32
4. The Most Important Teachers 59
5. Doing Nothing Is Teaching Too 70
6. Scars Run Deep 79
7. Help Before They Start to School 93
8. So You Have a Child in Grade School! . . 103
9. You Have to Believe in Something! . . . 124
10. Seeing Them Through to Maturity 137

To Teach A Child

To teach a child . . .
How could *I* have been chosen
For such a lofty task?
Two eyes look up and search my face.
Our eyes lock momentarily
And I feel the penetration,
Trying to see behind my eyes,
Trying to decide if love is there.
Two arms reach out.
Two hands clasp mine.
They seem to long for a firm grasp
That says, "Don't worry,
I know the way."
A warm heart beats close to mine.
Its metered cry is loud and clear:
"Love me. Love me. Love me."
How well I know that future days
Of loving and giving,
Or fear and withdrawing,
Depend upon the response
That cry hears now.
An eager mind holds up to me
The clay that forms the base
Of all future learning,
Begging, "Mold me . . . Mold me."
To teach a child . . .
No task more thrilling,
Nor yet more humbling.
God, grant me wisdom,
Grant me vision,
Grant me courage,
Grant me love,
To teach a child.

                              Ida Nelle Hollaway

1
It Takes All of Us

For days I had been watching Carla in my first grade classroom. Nothing that I or any of the children did seemed to appeal to her. She moved about quietly with a disinterested stare. From the total lack of response and participation she seemed to fit the pattern of the mentally handicapped child. Still, was there something in that quiet stare that indicated more, or was it just my incurable optimism again?

An incident on the playground helped me to understand. From the first day Carla had refused to mingle with the other children. She had chosen, instead, to stay in some corner of the playground alone. The children and I had tried several times to include her but each time she had run away. On this particular day she had chosen a bare spot of dry ground where there was a patch of heavy dust. When I noticed her she was sitting in the pile of dust, scooping it up with her hands and pouring it on her head. The dust was falling down her face and clothes, and she was making no effort to brush it aside. I went over to her and tried to speak quietly and without reprimand.

"Carla, you looked so pretty when you came to school this morning. Do you want to get so dirty that no one can see how pretty you are? Here, let me help you brush the sand off."

Carla kept right on scooping up the dust and pouring

it on herself. Finally, she blurted out, "I ain't nobody! We's all bad!"

Later I talked with my principal about the meaning of that statement. He told me that her two older brothers in our school had reacted to their poor start in life not as Carla had done with withdrawal but with aggression. They had been in trouble several times, though they were only eight and nine, and were, at the moment, suspended from riding the school bus for starting fights.

Carla was obviously accustomed to being lumped in with her brothers by her parents and others and classed "all bad." Since she knew within herself that she was not like them but nobody seemed to recognize that fact, she had concluded that she was a "nobody."

Anyone who has worked with young children will recognize that this had to be my starting point. We had to try to help her unlearn what her first six years had taught her before we could begin on anything else.

In the same class I had, by contrast, a happy, friendly, eager-to-learn, little girl named Shelley. She came tripping up to my desk one day and whispered in my ear, "You know what? You want to know a secret? Do you know how much I'm worth? My mommy said she wouldn't take a hundred million thousand dollars for me! And you know what else? You know that third grade reader you let me have? I can already read half way through it!"

I believe that the greatest frustration in teaching in the public schools in America today lies in the wide gap between the Carlas and the Shelleys in our rooms. In any given first grade this year there will most likely be those like Carla who cannot recognize a single numeral or letter of the alphabet or follow a simple command like, "Put it on the table." Right along beside them will be those, like Shelley, who can already read two years above their grade levels. But this is not the greatest problem. Greater than the problem of skills, or lack of them, is the problem of the children's self-concepts and the needs they present. We have the confident, eager, optimistic Shelleys put right along beside the defeated, loveless Carlas who have given up hope even before we begin.

So much is being said about accountability in our schools today. A great host of us are heartily in favor of accountability. Many of us spend an almost unbelievable number of hours each week trying to be as accountable as it is humanly possible to be. In the teachers' organization to which I belong, we have gone on record as favoring a system of accountability but preferring it be worked out within the profession by those who know the realities and goals of the classroom best. But every time we face a new class of first graders with its Shelleys and its Carlas, we have the definite feeling, We've started six years too late!

Now don't be perturbed. This is *not* going to be another of those guilt-producing attacks that places all of the blame for difficult children on the acts of the parents, whether those acts were premeditated, accidental, or unconscious. My thesis is, rather, that every child is a whole being and cannot be segregated into sections of home, school, and community. Our impact is on the life of the total child. If this impact is to be for his good, for the fullest reaching of his potential, then it should be a concerted, cooperative effort between his teachers in his home, his teachers at school, and all who touch his life in the total community.

One visit in the office of any one of hundreds of child psychologists would convince you that no one person or one set of circumstances produces most of our problem children. They are the products of a whole society which has in some way failed to meet their needs. How often the words are repeated, "Nobody cares for me." That means as the children search their young hearts and minds they cannot think of a relative, a neighbor, a teacher, a babysitter, a storekeeper, *anyone* they see each day or each week whose eyes, touch, or voice says to them, "I care about you. You are important to me."

In our society, with all of its rushing and crowding and lessened emphasis on families, churches, neighborliness, and society's increased emphasis on buying power and privacy and distrust, the children are often the losers.

One of the brightest children I have ever taught in my city was one of the most miserable. I taught him in both the first and second grades. He read far above grade level. Michael read all of the adult books his parents left lying around, appropriate or not. He read the voluminous *Jaws* five times in the first grade. He could quote long, gory passages verbatim to his classmates.

He often complained of the small amount of time he had with his parents. His father held down two jobs and his mother, three. One of hers was a night job at a truck stop miles from the city. Michael and his nine-year-old brother both had keys to their apartment and made many of the decisions on what to eat and which television programs to watch on their own.

I tried to talk to the mother. (The father never came to a requested conference or PTA program in the two years.) She assured me that all of the work they both did was "for the boys." There were so many things they wanted to give them she said. They recognized that they both had excellent minds and they were buying encyclopedias and saving for private schools and colleges. I

IT TAKES ALL OF US

tried to get her to see how much they needed *her* more than things.

I pointed out how bitterly disappointed Michael had been to miss a recent PTA program on which he had an important part. He reported that he had given her my note of explanation and had gotten himself all dressed and ready to go. Then she had come home and said she had a headache and couldn't take him. Michael had said to me, "But the real clincher was that fifteen minutes later, when it was too late for me to make the program, she got up and made my brother and me go to the carwash with her and help her wash the car!" Somehow, I couldn't seem to get through to her.

The next year when Michael was in the third grade his teacher came by to talk with me. A famous young entertainer had just committed suicide and most of the children seemed quite disturbed about it as they discussed it in their classroom. However, the teacher reported, Michael had simply shrugged his shoulders and said, "So what? That's probably the way I will end up some day."

When I asked him about it later, he gave a very matter of fact but sad reply, "Who would care?"

It is experiences like this that lead me to say that when we talk about accountability concerning our nation's children, we need to take a broader look than parents demanding efficiency tests for teachers or teachers blaming the home influences. We need to admit that building happy, useful, creative citizens requires a lot of accountability from all of us.

One of the frequent cries we hear today from the would-be problem solvers is "back to the basics!" While I'm well aware of the intended meaning of this phrase, something within me always wants to answer, *"Which* basics? Which of the basic needs of our children are being most neglected?"

In my research for graduate studies in education and in reading my educational journals with fair regularity, I have been impressed by the accounts of childhood education in such countries as England, France, Sweden, and the Soviet Union, as well as what I saw of the education and treatment of children in Japan during my sixteen years of residency there. I have come to feel that in all of these countries the children are nurtured and treated as a very important and precious part of the nation's resources more than in our own land. The populace in general seem to feel real joy in them and take time and effort to carefully instruct them in the meaning of things. For example, in Japan, I have marvelled to watch children walk through a city park to be smiled at by every adult they met and, more often than not, to also be spoken to quite gently. I have watched adults, even strangers, take time to look at a pretty stone with them, show them a butterfly, or listen with them to a bird or a locust.

In the schools in these countries I hear fewer reports of discipline problems. In some of these countries at least the obvious reason is the great respect for learning and the desire to excel. Of equal or greater importance is the belief instilled in them by their elders that they are important, contributing beings. I have also been impressed by the deep joy in music and art and their native literature that has been woven into their schooling. These things, along with the fact that increasingly the teaching of values and ethics formerly taught our children in their homes and churches has been left, instead, to our schools, and causes me to ask, *"Which* basics are receiving too little emphasis?"

However, we must admit there is some justification for those who, by their cry "back to the basics," mean a renewed emphasis on the "three r's: reading, 'riting and 'rithmetic." We were all rightly alarmed at news reports that twenty million Americans are functionally illiterate. My own family found this quite astounding, having returned here from Japan where the published literacy rate exceeds 99 percent.

Many have felt, perhaps rightly so, that the rebellious sixties grew out of some of the radical and nonprogressive currents of over-emphasis on open classrooms, freedom of choice, abandoning of grades, competition, and quality controls. These, wishing to stem the tide of over-permissiveness and lack of control have also found a voice in the "back-to-basics" cry.

However, in many instances, this honest cry of concern has been linked with too many others, less intelligent and less benign. One such group is those who call for autocratic discipline. In one county in Maryland, two school board members, who were up for reelection, based their campaign on the proposal to establish alternate schools that would stress the "three r's," enforce strict dress codes, outlaw the new math, and prohibit boys from growing their hair below the collar.

One group proposed to meet discipline problems by allowing students to walk in the halls only in silent, single-file lines under adult supervision from class to class.

An even more disturbing linkage, however, has occurred in some communities. Many public-minded citizens who are genuinely concerned about quality education have, without facing all that is involved, joined with people with little concern but their own pocketbooks who want to force budget-cutting at any cost upon public education. They cry loudly, "Cut out the frills," without stopping to realize what will be cut under such a policy. The first things to go will be art, music, librarians for elementary schools, physical education, school newspapers and journals, enrichment programs for gifted students, support programs for deprived students with an accompanying less emphasis on meeting the individual needs of the bright Shelleys and educationally and socially deprived Carlas.

These demands ignore three very important facts: (1) A child must *want* to learn before we can teach him even to read and write. How is this interest to be kindled if the rest of the curriculum is left so barren? Children want to learn when they see it as a key to many other skills that are interesting and rewarding, creative and artistic, such as drama, music, school newspapers, literature, books and magazines to read. When these are cut out as "frills" from where, then, is the motivation to come? (2) These demands ignore some of the most important contributing causes for the present deficiencies in basic skills. These deficiencies include a lack of emphasis on the printed word. Too few children today have patterns in their own homes and surroundings of parents and other adults who read *before* them, as one of the pleasures of life. Too many of them have parents (or sitters) who do not (or cannot) read *to* them from an early age as part of their daily diet and thus undermine good foundations for basic skills. (3) Some parents and some sitters use TV as a pacifier without helping to create a link between the programs the children view and reading and thinking for themselves and allow indescriminate viewing. True, sometimes they bewail the quality of the programs the children are seeing, but they fail to take any initiative to demand better material for the children.

In this regard, I recently read a report by a noted Amer-

IT TAKES ALL OF US 15

ican author who had visited in the Soviet Union with a large number of Soviet school children. In the course of the conversation she found the Soviet children appalled at the number of hours the American children watch TV and the types of programs they watch. All of the Soviet children present said they had TV sets in their homes but they had only three channels, mostly educational and cultural, with no advertisements and even so, there were only certain programs that children were allowed to watch.

The author said that when she returned to her hotel room she decided to watch a children's program. It was a program of poetry both by and for children. The poetry was recited from memory by children from various schools whose names and schools were announced. She admitted to cringing a bit as she thought of some of the violence and vulgarity our children were watching in America. In connection with this the author pointed out how the schools were involved with the whole communities, the homes, the libraries, the industries in molding and developing the character of the children. She stated that each year the standards of character to be met are very strictly defined and service projects in the community and in the school were worked out and well planned for achieving these goals, such as helping younger students, cleaning and repairing property, and group competition which utilized peer pressure to uphold approved standards of conduct.

In this book, as its name implies, I hope to take a look at our mutual accountability as parents, as teachers, and as citizens. By this I mean a look at the task, at the children whose growth we are trying to facilitate and at some of the ways we need to learn to cooperate if the outcome is to be optimistic.

I will not dwell on the tiny specifics (already too much discussed and made guilt producers in my opinion), such as, Did I wean her too soon? or Was I too pushy about his learning to walk, talk, or be toilet trained? Rather, I want to deal with the broader, more important issues, such as: What kind of self-image does he have? How secure does she seem? Has he learned to trust people and relationships? Is she paralyzed by unreasonable fears? Is he usually happy and enthusiastic? Have they learned enough beginning socialization to be willing to wait their turn, to rejoice in the success of others, and to help make group decisions? Are they still curious and creative? (Which assumes that all children are born with a certain amount of these qualities or they would not have learned to walk or talk or show affection.) Can she laugh easily? Is he ashamed to cry?

I have spent much of my last thirty-five years working with children at both ends of this spectrum. I have worked with children in Japan as a missionary for sixteen years. I have taught small children in the schools of America for over a decade. I have five children of my own, their births scattered over a fourteen year span. I also have six precious grandchildren.

I know what it is to feel the misery of guilt about some not-quite-definable omission or commission in our past because we took some "expert" too seriously or failed to follow our own gut-level inclinations. One of my hardest tasks in parent-teacher relationships today is working with the uptight parents who try too hard and cannot relax and just let their children *be* and *become*. However, there are some things that well-meaning parents do or fail to do because the deeper meanings have not been called to their attention. (Oh, that someone had told me!) There are many things they *could* do to facilitate the

IT TAKES ALL OF US

growth and learning of their school-aged children but no one has taken the time to explain them.

All across America today there are parents working as volunteer aids or as a "second right hand" to teachers as they help to make teaching aids or help to check the mass of work that piles up at the learning centers when eager children and challenging opportunities meet. There are, here and there, a few fortunate parents who meet weekly, or bimonthly with a teacher from their children's school for suggestions and instructions on how to prepare their preschoolers for the experience of public education. There are grandmothers, and other senior citizens as well as other community-minded volunteers finding much fulfillment in helping young children to grow and learn and mature and find meaning in our public schools.

That is what this book is all about. If the preschool home training can become a little more uniform so that the wide gap between the least prepared and the best prepared can be narrowed, every child in the room would benefit. If enough aid can be found for the classrooms, especially in the lower grades, to provide the one-to-one or very small-group training which some of the children need so desperately, it will free the teacher for more time to work with the gifted, highly creative children in the classroom.

For the moment, let's begin where all good teaching begins, with the child.

2
It's Me, Mom!

Every afternoon from September until June, several million doors swing open as children across America come in from school shouting, "It's me, Mom!" For the most part those cries will be heard as, "I'm home. I'm hungry. I'm through now and ready to play." And these interpretations will generally be right. But underneath those cries, for many there will be a more important, sometimes desperate plea, "It's *me!* Not just a loud kid who bangs the door. Not something else you have to *do*. Not a duty. Not a feather in your cap . . . or a millstone around your neck. It's *me!* Another human being wanting to be respected, to be listened to, to be accepted, and to be loved just as I am, just because I'm me."

Lots of those cries will be met with love and warmth and understanding. But every year, all year long, I worry about those who will not be met that way.

I firmly believe that nearly all parents, deep in their hearts, want their children to be happy, now and in the future. But what so many of them fail to realize is that happiness is not possible without self-esteem. I'm not talking about conceit and preoccupation with self, but self-acceptance, seeing ourselves as we are and liking what we see. It is a feeling of self-worth and significance so we don't have to waste time trying to impress people. Our self-knowledge of what we are gives the comfortable assurance that others will find out soon enough.

IT'S ME, MOM! 19

Yet as a first-grade teacher, every year much of the time I need to be teaching the so-called "basics" is taken up trying to change the poor self-concept of so many of the children who come to me. There is little real desire for achievement to build on without it.

For the last decade I have been teaching in a suburban school under court-ordered integration. I have been somewhat surprised to find that I meet this problem just as often from the so-called "good" homes of our neighborhood as I do from the inner-city homes.

I remember the day that Misty said to me, "I don't want to make a valentine. Aren't they supposed to say 'I love you' on them? Well, I don't love anybody and not anybody loves me." Her parents were divorced and both had married again to spouses with other children. She spent the weekdays in one home and the weekends at the other and felt like an intruder at both places.

Then there was the day we were writing a class poem about our mothers that many of the children had said they wanted to copy on a Mother's Day card when we finished. The children were taking turns thinking of reasons they loved their mothers. Valerie sounded like a rebellious teenager instead of a six-year-old when she spoke up.

"I don't know anything good to say about my mother, or my daddy either, for that matter. I don't see them very much. They are just sort of the zoo keepers, I guess you could say, they give us our grub and our orders on the way in and out."

Since neither of her parents, who had three beautiful little girls in our school, had come to any of the parent conferences, I sent home another urgent note asking if I could possibly see one of them.

Early the next morning, the handsome young father

came. He was obviously surprised and saddened by Valerie's remarks but his answer was, "I suppose that is a fairly accurate appraisal. You see, both my wife and I work and we only see the girls an hour or less apiece each day. Our business has long hours so my wife comes home and gives the girls a little supper, sees to their baths, and gets them into bed before she comes back for the night shift. She has a problem waking up early in the morning so I get up and give them some breakfast and get them dressed, their hair combed, and off to school. What else can I do?" he wanted to know.

"How long has it been since you have had a real, uninterupted, private talk with one of the girls?" I asked him.

"I can scarcely remember. When would I have time?" was his reply.

"The quantity of the time is not as important as the quality," I tried to tell him. "If you and your wife could arrange for even five really focused minutes a day with one of the girls, they would each get a turn four or five times a week."

He promised he would think about it.

How often I still think of the pale, nervous little Keith who would come into the room with signs of morning tears still evident. He liked to take his worksheet, fasten it on one of my clipboards, and get down on the rugs under one of the tables or off to himself in a corner to work. If I didn't keep a close eye on him he would work diligently for a few minutes then tear up the sheet and throw it away.

"I messed up," he would say with tears in his eyes.

Even the cafeteria workers noticed how up-tight he always was, counting and recounting his change for fear he would be a penny short.

"I've *got* to have it right," he would insist.

"What kind of mother must he have?" they asked me one day.

I didn't answer them, but later that day I thought Keith summed it up pretty well when he didn't want to take his math paper home.

"The trouble is," he said, "when she looks at my paper she never sees the eighteen I got right. She will just see those two I missed!"

I don't really know why I should choose Donny to tell you about, for I've seen the same thing happen over and over with other children and other parents. I guess it is because from the first day we went into the cafeteria Donny caught my eye. He had a pained look and seemed to have trouble carrying his tray. He bit on one lip and seemed to be concentrating very strongly on the whole process. I soon learned not to speak to him at this time because he seemed to resent my distraction.

Then one day his mother came to eat with him.

"Watch out, Donny! You'll spill it! You know you will!" she called out just as he started across the room.

"Why are you always so clumsy? Look what a mess you have made! You heard me telling you to be careful! You know how hard I've tried to get you to watch where you are going!"

So here was my obvious answer. Donny's mother's own self-esteem was very fragile. To her, that was all that was at stake. She couldn't even see the agony on Donny's face as he tried to wipe up the mess.

Between uptight parents who are so concerned with raising the perfect child, and the overworked or emotionally immature parent who have little time or emotional stamina to undergrid their children with the attention that would build their self-confidence, self esteem, I find this an ever-growing problem. Many of the parents are really trying. But somehow in all the rushed confusion of their lives, made worse by the mass media emphasis on perfect homes, spotless, harmonious, restful, peaceful, all presented as being so easy and entertaining but with little emphasis on the cost or responsibility involved, they miss the point that real happiness can *never* come apart from self-acceptance and self-respect. We are so created that we long to feel significant, worthy, needed. Where, then, do so many of our children run aground? Where have they missed that important ingredient of self-esteem?

Self-concept is based on the love or rejection a person encounters. A child's perception of himself is the reflection of the attitudes toward him of all those he meets.

Many psychologists believe this begins almost from the moment of conception, and that the emotional tone is set during the nine months in the womb by the health and well-being of the mother and her reaction to the pregnancy and the pain and inconvenience involved. So many young couples refer to "it" and never to "our baby" or "our child." If they could realize that in the first three weeks, by the time they have learned of its presence, the little heart is already beating its steady rhythm and its tiny organs are being formed, surely there would be less talk of abortions and less referring to "a person to be" and more talk and appreciation of "the person who already is."

For nine months the child is a part of its mother, its needs met by her by her constant pulse beat and presence. And then, suddenly, he is emptied out into a world, cut away from his parental part. He begins to explore, touch, search, look, and finds that he is a person. But what *kind* of a person he grows to feel himself to be will be based on the responses he receives from those about him. Body language will play an important part in the formation of this concept: how he is held, fed, bathed, has his diaper changed. Quickly he can sense whether he is endeared to those who care for him or is seen as a distasteful job to be performed. Very soon this acceptance or rejection reaches out into the community and everywhere he is taken. He searches faces and eyes watching for responses. Gradually his self-concept becomes his conditioned response to the way he is received in all situations, whether they are warm and delighted or cool and unfriendly. Thus the child's perception of the reflected attitude of those who comprise his world becomes the foundation for his own self or being. As he grows, self-concept is really his general anticipation of the rejection or acceptance he will receive in a given situation.

In a recent study in New York City, which included 175,000 people, it was reported that only 18.5 percent were free of symptoms of mental illness. Yet parents continue to spend much effort and money to be sure to prepare themselves with educational and vocational skills but few realize the great importance of training in the art of nurturing.

Since self-esteem is the pivotal point in successful, happy living, any question of accountability should begin here. Any child's judgment of himself has a great influence on the friends and work he chooses, how he gets along in school and in the community, the kind of person he marries, and how productive, stable, creative, and happy he will be. One of the greatest gifts that a parent, teacher, or friend can give to other people is to help them believe firmly in themselves and their worth.

Such belief or self-esteem must be based in two strong convictions: (1) I am lovable and matter and have value just because I exist, and (2) I have worth and have a definite contribution to make.

Those people who have worked with potential suicides or have studied this trend, especially the increased number of child and adolescent suicides in our nation, realize that the majority of those come back to this very point. Either they do not feel they *are* anyone of worth or they feel that what they are is not acceptable and is being destroyed. This point was indelibly impressed on my mind by a poem of a sixteen-year-old boy I found in *The Toronto Daily Star*. After writing these words he later committed suicide:

> He always wanted to explain things,
> But no one cared.
> The teacher came and spoke to him.
> She told him to wear a tie like all the
>   other boys.
> He said it didn't matter.
> After that they drew.
> And he drew all yellow and it was the
>   way he felt about the morning
> And it was beautiful.
> The teacher came and smiled at him.
> What's this? she said. Why don't you draw
>   something like Ken's drawing,
> Isn't that beautiful?
> After that his mother bought him a tie.
> And he always drew airplanes and rocket ships
>   like everyone else.
> And he threw the old picture away.
> And when he lay out alone looking at the
>   sky
> It was big and blue and everything

> But he wasn't anymore.
> He was square inside and brown
> And his hands were still
> And he was like everyone else.
> And the things inside him that needed
> saying, didn't need it anymore.
> It had stopped pushing.
> It was crushed.
> Stuff.
> Like everything else.

How, then, are we as parents, teachers, relatives, and friends, to help develop this all-important concept in the children in our homes, our community, and in our land? We should never hesitate for a moment to seek professional help either for ourselves or for the children when we doubt we are getting the task done. However, basically, here are ten important suggestions.

1. We must learn to accept ourselves. We cannot give what we do not have. We cannot truly accept others until we have accepted ourselves. Nurture comes from the overflow not from emptiness. The more you are fulfilled yourself the less danger there is that you will use the children to meet your own needs instead of seeking to understand and meet theirs. There is less danger, too, that you will take out your own insecurities on the child.

As our own feelings of personal worth develop, our ability to develop meaningful relationships also increases. Fortunately, this is a never-ending cycle. Our ability to build meaningful relationships with our children gives them strong self-concepts upon which they, in turn, can build such relationships. One of the greatest joys life has to offer is to watch the growth of self-esteem and relationships in grandchildren and great-grandchildren, being built on foundations you have been privileged to help lay in your own children. These foundations must be laid in an atmosphere of mutual trust and cooperation that helps all involved to feel loved, valued, and respected.

2. We need to feel and openly express the worth of *all* people as God's creation with specific purposes which only they can fulfill in this world. In the early days of integration in our nation, one of the saddest things I saw happen, and worked constantly to overcome, was some parents sending their children angrily to school armed with a barrage of advice on how to cope with their forced association with the "second-class citizens" who would be in their classes. Unless I could somehow circumvent that advice in *every* case, it would be the recipient of the advice who would suffer. None of us can believe that God creates second-class people without doing damage to our own self-concept. For it is when we can believe with Ethel Waters that "God don't make no junk" that we can keep rising above our own tendencies to second-class living.

3. We need to avoid critical or contemptuous attitudes that make a child feel worthless. Too often we fall into the bad habit of using certain words or cliches that undermine a child's sense of worth for a lifetime. "Stupid!" "How awkward can you get?" "You drive me crazy!" "Were you born in a barn?" "Don't you care about anybody but yourself?"

Sometimes people who fall into this habit are puzzled when their child seems unbothered when they do something which is obviously wrong. They should realize that when a child has been led to believe he is worthless, the normal reaction to follow is, What can it matter what I do?

4. Children need to be respected as individuals, as per-

sons in their own right. They deserve to be heard. I was impressed by a story Dr. Charles Allen told in his book *What I Have Lived By*. When he was pastor in Blue Ridge, Georgia, he was also the local scoutmaster. Among his boys was a big, overgrown boy with a seeming proclivity for getting into trouble and a reputation for being tough and hard. As a result, he was usually blamed for almost anything that was done wrong in the community. One day some wrong had been done and all of the boys began immediately to blame him. He stood by stoically as if waiting to be punished. Dr. Allen heard out all of the charges and then turned to the boy saying that now he wanted to hear his side. The big fellow broke down and cried.

"This is the first time," he said, "that anybody ever said I had a side."

If we treat children as individuals, we will expect the relationship to be reciprocal. As with other relationships, we should never anticipate they will be a one-way track. Children have a lot to contribute to our lives if given the chance.

Another aspect of respecting their individuality is respecting their right to own feelings. No feelings are wrong in themselves. Owning and admitting and verbalizing our feelings are the basis for an honest relationship. We should not say to a child, "No, you don't feel that way!" just because we do not approve. If, for example, a child says, "I just hate my sister," nothing is accomplished (but perhaps intensifying the feeling), by replying, "Now you know you don't feel that way!"

An empathetic response would be, "Sometimes other people really make us angry, don't they? Right now you almost wish you never had a sister."

Once his feelings are out in the open and are obviously

accepted by you, he will probably go ahead and tell you the cause of the feelings and they can then be dealt with, not denied. Denied feelings, however inappropriate, tend to smoulder and grow stronger. Sometimes great damage is done this way. For example, children are often quick to assume guilt for an illness or death of another person. If they have had recent ill feeling toward or have done something disrespectful to another, for example a grandparent, and then that person dies, they often feel responsible. Only when their relationship with an adult is of such a nature that they can verbalize this feeling of guilt can it be quickly and safely worked through.

5. We need to realize that neglect comes across to a child as lack of caring. This is not a feeling that is reserved for children. Anyone who has sat across the room from a spouse for an evening while that person read the paper or watched TV and has consistently gotten a detached nod or "Un-huh," to all questions or remarks, has to admit the feeling is quite normal. Of the children I have mentioned earlier in the book who have felt unloved, this has been the most common reason. Parents, for the most part—very well-meaning parents, have either been too busy or too absorbed in their own needs and have neglected to create an atmosphere of love and valuing and respect for their children. Parental neglect comes across to a child as a lack of caring or acceptance and leads to delinquent behavior.

6. We need to realize, also, that a lack of limit setting comes across precisely the same way. Little control makes a child feel uncherished. Too much control, or too much running interference to keep the child from being hurt, causes the child to feel untrusted, unworthy to face things on his own.

7. Consistency also is important. This is especially true

IT'S ME, MOM!

in the matter of verbal and nonverbal messages. Few things are more confusing to a child or to a young person than to be told one thing by our words and another by our eyes or face or body. For example, a child is told in words by his mother, "Certainly it is all right for you to make mud pies. It is OK to get dirty. Mother can wash your clothes." But at the same time her aversion to mud and all the guck shows clearly in her expression. The child gets the message, "Mother won't like you when you are all messy."

Sometimes, even our words give out double messages. For example a young college student asked his mother if it would be all right if he went on a camping trip with some friends in the Smokey Mountains. Her answer was something like this: "Of course you may go. You know I always want you to do the things that make you happy. Just be sure to remember how miserable I will be while you are gone. You know I will probably get a sick headache from worrying about you in those mountains. I probably won't get a wink of sleep until you get back."

What kind of happy answer could the young man find to such a confusing double signal? Inability to find happy solutions to such family relationships certainly does not help to build good self-concepts.

8. Constant lack of recognition, always being ignored, often causes a child to doubt his very being. I have watched mothers take a child with them to meet an adult for lunch and, without even introducing the child, go on visiting with their friend as if the child were not there. Sometimes they even go so far as to carry on a conversation about the child as if he were absent. Sometimes the child will make an effort to enter the conversation only to be promptly quieted as if he couldn't possibly have anything of importance to add to an adult conversation.

When a child is consistently ignored or treated as unacceptable, he feels overwhelmed and usually has one of two innate responses. Either he will attempt to reduce his world to a size that he can cope with, which usually means withdrawal, or he will fight to conquer and become very aggressive. He is very often pushed into this latter position when the parent leaves no "out" in the balance of power struggle or when the parent is always right.

9. We need to be careful not to promise more than we can deliver. We need to be as honest with children as we would be with any other human being. Circumstances and age and sensitivity need to be taken into account before we carry the honesty bit further than the young child is able to comprehend or accept. However, we should not glaze over the truth with false promises. They *won't* see their dead father again very soon. Everything may *not* be rosy tomorrow. The lost dog may *not* come home in the morning. Trust is one of the most important ingredients in building a relationship of love. And trust is based on honesty. Many times, for example, we can save a child a lot of worry if we admit our own mistakes or bad feelings honestly. If I say to a child, "I'm sorry I don't feel like talking just now. I've had a bad day and I have a headache. It has nothing to do with anything you have done. Is it OK if I rest a little while?" The child can then go on about his own business without worrying that the bad feelings, which he recognized anyway by my nonverbal communications, are not his fault and he doesn't need to worry.

10. We should be careful not to set too rigid standards. In the first place, since we are all human, these standards can never be reached. No matter how hard the child tries, he will always feel that it is never enough. Another ill effect of perfectionist standards is that those trained

under them come to expect the same thing of others and, therefore, they will always be disappointed.

When we consider how important to the total life of the child positive self-esteem is, surely we will want to do everything in our power to afford children a climate in which this self-esteem can flourish. As the famed Jersild pointed out, the best climate yet found for such flourishing is that suggested in the New Testament in 1 Corinthians 13: Faith, hope, and love. Faith that believes in the child, hope that holds great optimism for his future, and love that offers him total acceptance. We shall go into some of the deeper meanings of "the greatest of these" in the next chapter.

3
The Greatest of These

I have watched with interest, the growing popularity of writing personal marriage vows to be used in the wedding ceremony. I have been pleased to note how large a percentage of these, both from within and from without the Christian church, have chosen to include references to the characteristics of love as described in 1 Corinthians 13. As a worker with young children, the thought has crossed my mind so many times of how fortunate the future offspring of those marriages will be if the couples involved take seriously the need to build these very characteristics into the life-style upon which their children are going to depend for nurture.

The need for love in every human soul is rarely disputed in our day. In recent years empirical studies in a number of hospitals have lent acceptance to this fact by others than the theologians who have long felt it to be true.

When God created us, he put into each of us a longing for himself, the Creator. This longing is universal and leads men in all corners of the earth to a lifelong search for someone or something to fill this void. Oftentimes the longing becomes distorted and men seek fulfillment in power, sex, achievement, or other goals. But even when these goals are attained, the longing is still there. A longing for God is a longing for love. For God *is* love.

How then shall we describe the love for which all of

us long? The attributes mentioned above as being set forth in Corinthians offer an excellent answer. If all of us—parents, teachers, and friends—who vow our love for children were to display these attitudes toward the children, how much easier their development would be! Let's take a brief look at some of these.

Love is patient ("suffereth long")—Have you ever watched a young mother allowing her two-year-old to "help" her bring in the groceries from a shopping trip? She searches among her heavier loads for a small, light sack he can manage and then holds the car door open for him as he climbs out and gets a good hold on the bag. He walks across the lawn and he sets it down several times to "rest" or get a better hold on it. When he finally reaches the front steps, there is the long, slow process of trial and error to find out how you can use two hands to half crawl up the stairs and still have one left to hold onto the sack. Each step is a major accomplishment, as is the maneuvering through the door at the top of the steps. The mother stands there, holding her two heavy bags as she opens the door for him, knowing how much more quickly she could have carried all of the groceries inside and come back and carried her small son also. But love is patient. She wants to see him grow, master new skills, and learn the joy of helpfulness.

In the same way loving people will allow time and the indulgence of bungling trial and error periods for a child to grow, to experiment, and play. They will rejoice as they remember the person the child is becoming. By the time the first of our five children reached the "terrible twos" with all of the negative proclamations, I was well into the study of early childhood education and could see their constant no's as important steps in self-assertion and the havoc they sometimes played with my drawers and cabinets as aiding their valued inquisitiveness and their need for exploration. However, I wish now that someone had helped me to see adolescence in much the same light, as a time for rejoicing over the growth that was taking place. I wish I could have seen the countless hours my teenagers spent on the phone as an important search for validation and identity. I wish I could have seen their cluttered, junky rooms as a drive for independence and selfhood. When they argued and "talked back" to us, I wish I could have been happy at the evidence of self-assertion and efforts at discrimination and decision making on their own. If I could have seen through eyes of love (and enlightenment) a little more often, perhaps I could have shown a little more the patience of love.

Most of the adults who touch the lives of small children need more of this quality. Perhaps we would allow children more time to "do nothing" so they could know peace and self-study and the joy of being alone. I notice that much of the propaganda for smaller families stress the advantages to an only child in having so much more of his parents' attention. I remember so well that one of the advantages of being a part of a busy, larger family is that you *escape* some of that attention. You can close your bedroom door without anyone feeling you are shutting them out. Actually, they are probably more often relieved that you are shutting yourself in! You can disappear up into a tree house or down into the meadow without anyone coming to look for you, while you spend long, delicious hours just daydreaming or figuring out the whys of things.

If love is patience, perhaps it would help us if we could see impatience as unlove. We would certainly resist the temptation to waste so much of our time and effort trying to hurry children. "Hurry and bathe. Hurry and get to bed. Hurry and go to sleep. Hurry and get up. Hurry with your dressing. Hurry and brush your teeth. Hurry and eat. Hurry, it's time to leave. Oh yes, don't forget to hurry home!" This perpetual hurry game seems to go on day in and day out in many homes.

Another kind of insidious impatience has to do with the rate of growth. Many adults are overly eager to see that a child passes each milestone of development on or before the time of the mythical average child of his age, according to some developmental chart or book. How agitated they become if the child becomes six-months-old without cutting a tooth or sitting alone or a one-year-old without attempting to walk or the age of two without talking.

When the child enters kindergarten or first grade, there are more ways to compare them with their peers and more skills to check on the lists of "normal behavior."

I always remember little Monette when I think of all of this. After about two weeks in the first grade, Monette began trying to prolong the school day. She seemed to dread going home every afternoon and begged to stay a little longer. At first I flattered myself that she was really enjoying school, but there seemed to be more to it than that. Finally she came out with the real reason in an obviously tense question, "Mrs. Hollaway, when am I *ever* going to learn to read? My mother meets me at the door every afternoon, waiting to ask me, 'Monette, have you learned to read yet?'"

I should not have been surprised for it is a battle first-grade teachers fight every year. Anxious parents ask their children, day after day, "What did you learn today? Aren't you learning anything? Did you write anything? Did you count? Have you begun on the workbook I bought? Did you learn any new words? When are you going to start learning? Don't you do *anything* but *play?*"

How often I have wished they could be patient. June is a long way off and besides, play is learning! The first few weeks we are more interested that the children learn to like school, that they learn to listen and follow directions, that they become enthusiastic about learning, and that they build an atmosphere of sharing and helping each other to learn. Impatient parents and families make all of this harder by causing the children to feel that they are disappointing them by not learning as fast as they should. The children know this is not their fault, and so become disenchanted with the very process I am trying to help them enjoy. A little patience would help a lot!

Love is not self-centered ("seeketh not her own")—If you sit in a public lounge or tearoom, or often in your own livingroom, and just listen to a group of people talking, it usually doesn't take you long to be reminded how self-centered we human beings are. Most of us are only half listening, and that for one obvious reason: to find a break in the conversation just long enough that we can jump back in with our *own* opinions or stories of our *own* lives.

Too much self-centeredness in the adults attitudes toward a young child may indicate some dangerous expectations which should be avoided.

(1) The child should not be expected to satisfy the unmet needs of the adult. This is often attempted in several different ways. Adults who are over-anxious about their child's rate of growth and achievement often may feel they were shortchanged in attention and praise and hope to receive it vicariously through their child. The same kind of vicarious enjoyment or accomplishment often is sought by the parent who tries to make the child into

something he or she failed to become: a football player, a pianist, a singer, ballet dancer, or whatever. Another unmet need of the adult by which the child is sometimes victimized is the need for affection. We have already talked of the need for normal affection in the home, but the mother, whose normal needs in this area have been unmet, will often try to bind the child too closely to herself instead of progressively freeing him to become his own person, which is the nature of true love.

(2) The child should not be expected to be a carbon copy of the adult. This happens in the area of vocational choice, which is somewhat understandable but still unreasonable. It also happens in the area of personality or being, which is entirely impossible. Sometimes the child is the very opposite type from the parent and any attempt to press for similarity can lead to a deep wound. A friend of mine bore such a wound for many years because his father told him as a teenager, "Son, you have no personality." He was a mature man before he realized that his father meant, "Son, you don't have a personality like mine." The father was a fairly loud, outgoing showoff. The son was a quiet, pensive, sensitive boy. For many people his personality was much more pleasing than his father's, but that was not the message the boy received. For a long time he felt that he was substandard or insufficient just because he was different.

(3) The child should not be expected to fit a preconceived idea of the parent as to the kind of child they hope to have. A girl in the same graduate school with me was almost destroyed by this demand from an otherwise loving father. He had wanted more than anything to have a son. His first child *was* a son, but he did not fit any of his father's ideas of what a son should be. He was quiet, artistic, and intellectual and cared nothing for

what his father felt it took to be a "real man, a man's man." Later, when his daughter was born, she seemed to be the active, outdoor type he had desired in a son. So he proceeded to train her to fill the place of the dreamed-of son. He taught her to ride and train horses, to hunt, and to fish. He was very happy with the arrangement, but the girl almost lost her identity as a female.

At the university this girl met and fell in love with a young man. But for a long, long time she could not bring herself to promise to marry him. She was afraid of her role as a female. It took months of counseling by a patient psychologist for her to be willing to make such a commitment. Eventually they were married and moved away from her father and her former life. Everything seemed to go reasonably well for a time. However, after a year of two she called the psychologist in a flood of tears. She seemed terribly distraught. The reason?

"I'm pregnant!" she cried. "How can I ever possibly be a mother?"

Once again the terror of her role as a female was robbing her of what should have been some of her happiest moments.

Love is gentle ("not easily provoked")—We hear a lot about the "battered child" today, and such physical abuse *should* be exposed, the child rescued, and transferred to more loving care. However, some of the most intense suffering comes to the psychologically abused children. Uncontrolled anger is often behind both of these abuses.

I remember how mistaken I was when I first tried to determine why John Alan got sick so often. He seemed timid and afraid, and I thought that perhaps immaturity and lack of proper preparation had made starting to school too much for him. I talked to his mother about it and her reply was quite enlightening.

THE GREATEST OF THESE 39

"Naw, that ain't it," she insisted, "He's always been sickly, especially when his dad's at home. George, he has a real bad temper and he ain't got much use for kids. He yells at John Alan a lot and John Alan spits up a lot. His dad says he does it on purpose, like it was his way of talkin' back."

After that I watched John Alan more closely. Two conditions seemed to provoke his sick stomachs most often: if someone showed anger or if he did not understand what was expected of him. Because he was so tense, it usually took more instructions for him, more carefully and quietly given, than for the other children.

When my pastor told the following story of a little retarded boy and his sister, it reminded me of John Alan.

The little boy had wandered into a drug store. Seeing a bottom shelf with a row of bottles on it, the little boy sat down on the floor beside the bottles and started lining them up on the floor to play with them. When the druggist saw what he was doing, he asked him to stop, but with no response. The druggist yelled at him to stop and told him to put the bottles back in their place. The little boy didn't seem to hear and went right on with his playing. The druggist yelled more loudly, but still he was ignored.

About that time the boy's sister, who had been looking for him, heard the druggist and came running into the store.

"Please, Mister," she told the druggist, "he doesn't understand that kind of talk."

She went over and sat down beside her brother and talked to him very quietly. In a moment he picked up all of the bottles, put them back on the shelf where he had found them, and started silently out of the door.

"What did you say to him? How did you get him to

do it?" the druggist asked the little girl.

"Oh, I just sort of love it into him," she replied.

It's not only the retarded children who need that kind of treatment. All children thrive on it. Love is gentle.

Love sees the good ("rejoiceth not in iniquity, but rejoiceth in the truth" or as the Revised Standard Version has it, "does not rejoice in wrong, but rejoices in right")—When I read those words I think of little Keith, the fearful little boy I mentioned earlier who said his mother never could see the eighteen problems he got right for looking at the two he got wrong. I think children have an innate knowledge that this is *not* love.

But there is a knowledge which has come to be recognized by many that I find myself wishing so often were innate to all adults who profess to love children. It is the knowledge that remarks made about children in their hearing often become self-fulfilling prophecies. I shudder to think of some of the negative ways parents have introduced their children to me when they have entered first grade. Sometimes they are joking. More often they are serious. But I believe that in most instances the child took the words at face value. Here are just a few:

"I feel sorry for you. You are going to have your hands full with Reagan. He just drives me up the wall."

"I just wanted to warn you. Never presume that Brad hears anything until you say it at least three times. Oh, he *can* hear. I've had him tested. He just prefers not to, I think."

"I came by to bring you Christy's lunch money. I could never trust her to get it all the way from the front door, down the hall to this room without losing it. She loses everything. If you ever send me a note by her, or anything that is important, you had better pin it to her dress and then call me to see if I got it."

"I'm sorry to tell you but you sure are going to have a harder time with Greg than you did with his brother. He just never has been as bright somehow."

"My, what a pretty room! I hope you don't have many like my Mickey or they will make short work of it. He tears up everything in sight."

"Boy, am I glad to see you! If this summer had been one day longer I would have lost my mind. When Penny gets so loud you just can't think, try to imagine what it would be like to spend the whole summer with three just like her!"

I could go on and on. But I always wonder to myself how often the child has heard this. I wonder, too, what chance I have of overcoming the acceptance these children have already given to these views of their selfhood.

Of course there are some refreshing memories of mothers or dads who have come in with positive, reassuring words. I remember when Mrs. Anthony said, "Here's my little delight, Beth Ann. You two are going to enjoy each other. You have so many nice things for children to do and Beth Ann just enjoys doing everything!" I looked at the mother's enthusiastic, loving face and thought to myself, "I just bet she does. I think that would probably be true of any child of yours."

Another mother put it this way, "Isn't this an exciting day! Jan and I have been looking forward to it for so long. She's going to make you a great first grader. She's so quick to learn and such a good helper. You both are very lucky."

I remember Jack's daddy too. "I don't know how I am going to spare this little guy. He helps in my shop and helps at home and helps keep everybody on our street happy. But I don't want him to miss the fun you are going to have here. I'll see you this afternoon, Jack.

He's a real winner, Mrs. Hollaway."

Self-fulfilling prophecy. I said I worried about how I would keep the first prophecies from coming true. However, I doubt I could have done anything to have stopped this last set if I had so desired. Someone believed in those children. Someone had seen the good in them and had prophesied it would win. And it did, and it will!

Recognizing the good in children is one of the greatest gifts we can give to them. But there is another gift just as precious. That is the gift of seeing the good in all people everywhere. Sympathy, tolerance, brotherhood, and faith in all mankind grow out of this gift.

When desegregation orders were first handed down to my section of America, I did not agree with all of the provisions and the inequitities included, but I did agree with the intention behind them—to give meaning to the basic tenets of this nation that all men *are* created free and equal. Like a lot of other idealistic Americans, we faced a lot of dark days as we began to see revealed what a lot of our children are being taught in the homes of our nation.

I remembered how my children had learned the song, "Carefully Taught," from the Rogers and Hammerstein musical, *South Pacific* while we were overseas. They were enjoying the wonderful privilege of attending school with forty-six nationalities.

They were puzzled by the meaning of the song that prejudice is handed down in families and in social groups, that children must learn at an early age to hate people who are different from themselves. To them, all of this was so foreign to their own natures and experiences, it was hard for them to conceive of it.

I'm sorry to say it didn't take long after our return to America and several incidents, such as the burning of a cross in our yard when one of our boys befriended a black girl at his school, for them to learn rapidly that such is actually possible. Some children *are* very carefully taught.

As the refrain of that song runs through my mind, I realize anew the truth of the words as I listen to children who had been "carefully taught" in contrast to those who were following their own natural inclinations.

During that first year of desegregation my first graders had to pass through ugly lines of demonstrators, making angry threats, and carrying indecent signs to get into their schools. Many of them came to school puzzled by the instructions they had received at home. White children asked, "Why did my daddy tell me nobody could make me sit by a black child?" or "What did my parents mean when they said not to take nothin' off of no nigger? Did they mean don't steal nothin' from them?" Black children asked, "Why did Daddy say, 'If a white boy hits you, knock him down'?" or "Why did Mother say 'You make them leave you alone'?"

I kept all of the desks and chairs turned away from the window and tried harder than usual to keep the attention of the children on the joy of laughing and listening and sharing. I tried harder to make of our group a caring whole which would add to the life of each child there and help them to transcend some of the things they were being "carefully taught."

It is only fair to add that my task was made easier by the presence of some children who had been taught acceptance and love which did not draw boundaries. They had been fortunate to be brought up in homes where the prevailing attitude was one of this accepting love instead of tension, fear, and suspicion.

Before I leave this matter of self-fulfilling prophesies,

I think it is important to point out the tremendous effect of teachers, church workers, and the larger community in this area.

Year after year I see small children who have "gotten off on the wrong foot" in their social interaction. They are not as friendly as some would like or as quick to respond. Some are awkward in their body movements and bump into things and often knock something over. Some of them are loud and seem to tend to push other children around. They seem to be a little slow in grasping what is expected of them in various circumstances. Before long the community, sometimes teachers or neighbors or storekeepers or even church workers, begin to label them as "troublesome" or "naughty" or even "mean." I always cringe when I see this happening because I know how often these children grow up trying to live up to their reputations.

I often think of Annette when she was in my third grade in the all-black school. She was quite intelligent but was an assertive, often bossy, sometimes belligerent little girl. Her home situation, with too much responsibility placed on her eight-year-old shoulders, had made her that way.

We liked each other from the beginning. Little by little she began to let me see through the crack in the heavy shell of self-defense that surrounded her. She lived in a small trailer with her mother and five younger children, the youngest of whom were eight-month-old twin boys. One morning Annette showed up at school several minutes early to show me something she had brought. She said she had not gotten her math assignment and she thought that if I read the list of things her mother had left for her to do when she got home from school the day before, maybe I would understand why she had been unable to do her math assignment.

She handed me the list:

Wash diapers for the twins
Take twins and Lynn and Dody outside for some air
Wash and boil baby bottles
Feed twins cereal and fruit
Fix kids supper (Soup and sandwiches will do)
Send Paul (the five-year-old) to the store for milk
Bathe kids. Paul and Eddie can do themselves, the rest needs help
Fill baby bottles with milk
Put three big kids to bed
Feed twins and put to bed
Wash supper dishes
Fold the diapers

She watched me as I read the list and then she added: "Just as I 'bout got through, 'bout eleven, Cynthia waked up and started cryin'. I had to lay down beside her to keep her from wakin' up the rest, and I guess I was tired 'cause I accidently fell asleep. So, see, I couldn't get my math."

I mentioned her plight to some of the other teachers and the reply I got was almost unanimous, "She won't ever amount to anything. Bad blood."

I tried to tell them that was impossible. *Everybody* amounts to *something,* good or bad. With her intelligence and forced early maturity, we had better hope Annette amounted to something good, I insisted, or the community would have its hands full one day.

Last year I was visiting in that community and one of the older teachers stopped me to say, "Do you remember Annette and what you used to say about her? Well she's amounted to something bad all right. Let me tell you about her latest escapade."

It seems that Annette, at fourteen, had a baby almost a year old. She looked eighteen and passed as an adult. She had come to the school a few times to look around and, as the teacher put it, "to case the joint." She discovered that one of the special education teachers had to personally escort some of her children to the bus every afternoon. The others, already prepared to leave, had to wait alone in their seats for the teacher to return.

One day, just as the teacher left the room with the first group, Annette appeared, dressed like a teacher, and walked confidently into the room.

"Boys and girls, get out your paper and pencils," she announced, "I want you to work the problems I am putting on the board."

"But our teacher done tole us to put 'em away. It's time for the bus," they protested.

"Your teacher was called away, and I'm your substitute teacher. I said get out your pencils and paper and get to work," Annette commanded confidently.

The children complied while Annette sat down at the desk and accomplished her mission. She left before the teacher returned.

"What in heaven's name are you doing?" the teacher asked as she came back into the room. "I thought I told you to be ready for that bus!"

"Yessum, you did," they replied. "But the substitute tole us to get 'em back out an' do that boardwork."

"What substitute?" the teacher asked incredulously.

"The same one that got your purse out of the desk and took out all of your money and credit cards," the children replied.

The story struck me as a bit comical at first but later I felt a sadness about it all. I remembered my dreams of the person Annette could have been, except for the circumstances and all of the self-fulfilling prophecies. There were simply not enough people who "rejoiced not in iniquity, but rejoiced in the good." A child who could, at the age of eight, complete that long list before she slept could have done so many wonderful things.

Love is strong. ("beareth all things . . . endureth all things")—Real love has the strength to undergird the life of the one loved. The kind of nurture and help others need in times of discouragement or strife or grief requires a measure of maturity and self-strength on the part of the would-be helper. Many parents, for example, do not realize how often they do more harm than good in this area when they have not squarely faced their own needs and inadequacies. This causes them to see things out of perspective. They feel personally threatened by the mistakes or problems of their children. Sometimes this results in refusing to accept the children's feelings or even allowing the children the right to *have* feelings.

"You don't feel that way. You know you don't," they insist. "Nice girls don't want to go off alone. Nice boys don't hate *anyone!*"

Or they become angry and defensive with, "You can't possibly think of doing that. After all we've done, are you going to disgrace us all? I'm so hurt and ashamed."

Or again, the defensive adult may become very domineering, "I will not have that kind of talk in my house. Go to your room. No more car, no more TV, no more allowance, or privileges until you can think straight and talk straight." (Which is, being interpreted, "Until you can think and talk as I do.")

It takes an inner peace and strength on the part of

adults to face such times with equanimity and love and justice. Such inner peace would allow them, first of all, to *listen*. Too many adults, I fear, fail to listen, but pounce right in on the child with advice, warnings, and incriminations before they have been willing to hear them out. The more mature person, who is able to keep things in proper perspective, will hear the child or young person out, try to understand what they are saying and try to empathize with their feelings. How wonderful (albeit how unusual, I fear), if the adult could say, "I can see you are upset. I can see this is a hard situation for you. I know that it is probably hard for you to believe I could understand or be of any help, but I *do* love you and want to help anyway I can. I want to hear how this makes you feel and what you think we should do about it."

One minister's wife found that being able to handle a very difficult situation in her daughter's life with love and understanding permanently changed her relationship with her daughter. It also led to some about-faces in the somewhat confused life of her daughter.

The minister's wife came home from work one day to find an agitated husband waiting for her. The young man who had been seeing their daughter for several months and who was in most ways they thought, a fine young man, had come to the husband's office that day to tell some disturbing news. He wanted her father to know that he had gotten his daughter pregnant out of wedlock. He said he loved her and was willing to marry her or do whatever she desired, but she was very upset and confused about what they should do. For a whole week she had been talking intermittently of an abortion, but she always ended up in crying.

The parents decided they should drop all of their plans for the evening and drive to the college town and see their daughter. They knew that although the relationship had been somewhat strained of late, their daughter loved them and was probably worried about their reactions.

When they arrived in the university town, they went to the address where they had been told their daughter was living. The apartment which they had supposedly been paying rent on all year was occupied by strangers. The young girl there, embarrassed at being called out of a boy's bed, nevertheless told them how to get to their daughter's boyfriend's apartment, suggesting that he might know where their daughter was.

They found the way to the apartment but by now it was well past midnight. They knocked on the door repeatedly but got no answer. As they knocked, the door came ajar a bit so they cautiously pushed it open and stepped inside. They saw immediately that the breakfast set was the one they had given their daughter. Her dishes were in the cabinet and in the sink. No one needed to spell out the meaning.

They went to the door of the only bedroom, knocked, and called their daughter's name. When she answered softly, they cracked the door just enough to realize that the two were in the bed. They asked them if they would like to slip on something and come into the other room for a short talk.

When the daughter walked in, tear-stained and fearful, the mother opened her arms to receive her and said simply, "I just had to come and tell you how much I love you."

"*You* love *me?* Like this . . . you love *me?*" she asked with sheer amazement.

As they embraced, the mother whispered, "Of course I love you. We both do, very much. But we didn't come to talk of the past. We will talk of the future, if you like, and about that new little person who has come to join us."

The daughter's face began to glow. "Then I *can* have him. I don't have to talk about abortion any more! We *can* get married and make a home for him."

The mother says that as far as she and her daughter are concerned that night began a new relationship for them. She also says that so often, when the two of them look at that adorable little boy who blesses the whole family with his brightness and his mirth, they think of that night when love made all the decisions.

It isn't always easy but it is certainly more than worth the effort. Love is meant to be strong.

Love has a positive sense of direction. ("believeth all things, hopeth all things")—We have just had two illustrations of this attribute of love or the lack of it. The minister's wife was able to salvage something very wonderful through positive hope and belief. Annette's life was turned in the opposite direction by the lack of such concern.

I remember hearing one man tell of the positive set which his father had given to his life. It is best illustrated, he said, by a scene when his father was trying to help him learn to ride a bicycle. Like most of us, he had kept watching the bicycle and the ground beneath him. His father kept calling out, "Keep looking up, Son. Keep looking up!"

That scene, he said, was typical of his father and his great contribution to his son's life. He had always been standing by to keep him reminded to keep looking up.

To keep a cheerful eye on the present, believing the best about a child, and an optimistic eye on the future, hoping for all the good things his eventual fulfillment will bring, is a wonderful gift to give a child.

Optimism is catching. I remember the little boy in my class named Shawn who I always called Mr. Optimism. I was tempted to play games with him, just to see if I could say something discouraging enough to bring forth a less than optimistic answer. Our days went something like this:

> "Sorry, Shawn. It's raining. We can't go outside."
> "Great! We'll get to play checkers!"
> "Oh, Shawn. It has stopped raining. We'll go out after all."
> "Hot ziggety! Football!"
> "Shawn, you have to do this math over. You were careless with your regrouping and missed eight of them."
> "Wow! I got two more right than yesterday!"
> "Our trip for the theater tomorrow has been cancelled. They said they'd try to work us in next month."
> "Boy, oh boy! May is a great month for a field trip!"

I really felt he was one of a kind until I got his little brother, Andy, two years later. I couldn't believe my good fortune, Mr. Optimism No. 2!

As I became better acquainted with their parents, I could understand why they were always so happy. It was a family trait. Optimism is caught. Unfortunately, negativism is also caught. Thankfully, a negative first grader is a rarity. But I have never taught one that did not confirm my immediate suspicion that he came from a negative home.

I have a friend who has a negative mother. I've heard her grandchildren say. "Oh Grandmother, thank you for the good angel food cake you made."

Her response, "It's high time you said something about it!"

Her daughter said, "The leaves and flowers are getting so pretty. I would like to take you for a ride."

"Now what makes you think that *I* have time to fool around like that with all I've got to do?" came her reply.

For my friend, this negativism resulted in a very poor self-concept. Since there was always much criticism and very little praise, she always felt that no matter what she did it was never enough.

She hated being treated that way and felt desperate to get out in a home of her own. She married and had three lovely children.

The result? Too much of the time she finds herself repeating her mother's actions. She is often critical, suspicious, demanding, and rigid. Such attitudes are caught.

The cycle continues. Her children, now in their late teens, are anxious to leave home for fear it will be continued in their homes some day.

We need to teach our children that it is not the circumstances that control our lives but how we interpret and react to them. Potentially bad happenings can bless our lives if we take a positive attitude that we can learn and grow from the trials. Likewise, good things become bad if misused and misinterpreted. If we could but face every day "believing all things" and "hoping all things," both we and those around us would be unusually blessed.

Love can be trusted, relied upon. ("love never faileth")—The importance of trust in our lives and in the lives of our children can scarcely be overemphasized. All relationships, friendships, marriages, working relationships are only successful to the extent they can be based in trust. It is impossible to build a confident, happy life without trust in one's own self and in others.

The opposite of trust is fear. Most people are aware of the words, "Perfect love casts out fear" but many of them do not realize that love does this by building a base of trust. There can be no fear at all in a relationship which knows perfect trust.

Most small children build their first base of trust while they are still infants. In the first year of life most of their needs are met quickly and pleasantly. They are fed when they are hungry. They are changed when they are wet and uncomfortable. They are held and comforted when they are upset. Thus it is easy for them to develop trust in their world. Children who do not have these needs met develop an awesome fear. Sometimes their fear, like that of a frightened, mistreated animal, is pitifully obvious. For some of them it brings withdrawal and even retardation.

But even some of that majority of children who come through this early period relatively unmarked by fear or lack of trust encounter such all too soon.

Trust comes through consistency. Many psychologists have expressed the belief that even relatively poor or insufficient care, if consistent, is better than a higher level of love and care which cannot be depended upon. In like manner, many educationalists agree that some of the poorer forms of discipline, although harsh and sometimes painful, if rendered with consistency, may be easier for a child to assimilate than some better forms rendered inconsistently. The child needs consistency to know what he can count on. He wants the boundaries well-defined. This is an important element in building trust. Even adults have a hard time dealing with constant change and inconsistencies. But we have had time to build up some inner resources for processing them and transcending them. This is not true for a child. He is just now trying to build those inner structures and thus finds such things extremely difficult and confusing.

A child also needs to feel that he is trustworthy, that someone believes in him. One "I am counting on *you*" can be worth a hundred "You had better do it my way." Many successful people say repeatedly that one of the biggest factors in their lives has been having someone to believe in them.

One word of caution, however. Don't overdo the buddy bit with your children. Be yourself. Don't be afraid to be an adult. The children know the difference and they want *you*, not some idea of what you think they need. They need you as a model.

One little boy who had been spending the day with his father, supposedly "having fun," was found in his room alone on his bed, crying.

"Why, Jimmy," the mother exclaimed, "What in the world is the matter?"

"I spoiled Daddy's whole day," he wailed. "I don't want to go any more."

"What do you mean, Honey?" his mother asked.

"We went swimming and he spent the whole time in that little old shallow pool with me. I know he wanted to dive off the big diving board in the deep water, and I wanted to see him, but he didn't do it. He just stayed with me and pretended to have fun. Then when we went to lunch he ordered a hot dog just because I did, but he kept watching the man at the next table with a steak. But the worst was when we went to the park. He didn't get to sit down and watch the pigeons like he always likes to do with you. He thought he had to help me ride the merry-go-round. It was awful."

"But he was just trying to be a pal to you," his mother explained.

"But I've got lots of pals," Jimmy replied. "All I want is a Daddy!"

I think one other word of caution is important here. *Don't fake it.* Expressing love that you do not feel, love that you do not put into action that a child can feel and understand, does more harm than good. It gives a negative concept of love.

One little girl who was being treated in a home for disturbed children defined parent love as the kind that picks you up and kisses you and then puts you down and goes off and leaves you. By contrast she expressed affection for one of the therapists because, as she put it, "she be-cares me." To find a way to express the meaning of one who shows love in action she had to coin her own word, "be-cares" me, because love, as she had experienced it, did not fit.

The somewhat amusing but pitiful story is told of a woman who consulted a psychiatrist about her "incorrigible" little daughter. After working with the child a while the psychiatrist told the mother that the child desperately needed love.

"Love?" the mother is said to have replied. "Why I tell that brat three times every day that I love her!"

Children must feel loved before love, the abstraction, has any meaning for them.

Many teachers of children in the lower elementary grades find that they can spot certain children as winners almost from the very first day. Almost invariably they are children who have this strong sense not only of being loved but also of being trusted, counted on to do well. Some of them, like Ethel Waters, have been taught from an early age that "God don't make no junk" and that both their families and their God are expecting them to find the purpose they were created for and then to excel in it.

None of us can see our own faces, except in a mirror.

We see ourselves, most often, in the mirror of the eyes and the attitudes of people around us. If those mirrors tell a child that he is worthy and useful and loved, he grows in self-trust.

A child also needs to see love and trust evidenced in the relationships of those he loves, who are of prime importance to him. To live with parents who obviously love and trust each other will leave an indelible mark on his young life.

Unfortunately, those who quarrel constantly, express nontrust when they are angry, or bicker and find fault when they feel hurt or rejected also leave a deep mark on the child. If those he loves most cannot be trusted, why should he look further? For this very reason, many persons have found that real faith in God is difficult for them because of the words "heavenly Father." Their experience with an earthly father has left them confused, hurt, and distrustful. This sometimes makes them unable to feel trust at any level.

This fact is very crucial, especially in a religiously oriented person, because God is the only completely trustworthy being any of us will ever know. He alone is eternal, always there, constant and consistent, unchanging and unfailing. He is the ultimate source of validation, love, and trust. It is extremely unfortunate when a child has found so little of these characteristics on a human level that, as he grows older, he finds it almost impossible to accept them on the divine level.

Love above all else ("but the greatest of these is love")— While it is true that all of the characteristics we have been discussing are attributes of love, so, basically, they *are* love. It seems appropriate that we end the chapter as the Corinthian letter did, by saying that no matter what else we may give a child in either material or spiritual gifts, no gift can compare with the gift of love. Nothing can contribute more to his security, inner peace, self-image or well-being.

On the other hand, nothing destroys all of these more quickly or more devastatingly than fear. This problem of fear is so prevalent today that it can scarcely be overemphasized.

Psychologists often have listed the three most prevalent fears among young children as: fear of loss of approval; fear of abandonment; and fear of loss of love.

Fear of loss of approval includes the fear of failure. This often freezes the individual into a state of nonaction. It can bring many forms of distortion in thinking and life, according to the demands of the one the individual is seeking to please. For example, if that person is very rigid and bound by the letter rather than the spirit of the law, the young person may find himself bound by an impossible perfectionism in attempt to please for fear of losing approval.

Fear of abandonment may be related to separation by divorce, work, or even death. The parent should be aware that many children's questions about death may really be questionings and fears around this matter of abandonment. When Bobby asks, "Why did Grandpa die? Will he not ever come back any more?" He may really be asking, "Are you going to die? Are you going away and leave me like Grandpa did?"

Fear of loss of love, of course, encompasses both of the first two. One of the cruelest results of divorce, especially when it occurs before the child is six, is that it makes this particular fear so great that it is often difficult for some persons *ever* to trust themselves to love again.

I have tried to point out repeatedly that the answer to fear lies in love. Likewise, the answer to a positive self-image, the ability to trust, the optimism of hope that sees the good, the practice of patience, the possibility of losing self-centeredness in the common good, the strength to believe and to endure, all lie in love.

4
The Most Important Teachers

It is rare in America to find parents who do not include an education for their children somewhere near the top of their list of priorities. What do they mean? Where do they expect to get this desirable, essential ingredient for their children's future?

Most of them would answer immediately, "In our schools," whether public or private. They seem to feel that most of the things their children need should be neatly packaged and delivered to them between the hours of nine and three during less than half of the days in a year. The word *educate* came from the Latin word *educare* which means "to rear." This in itself seems odd because the word *education* has, through the centuries, come to mean the acquiring of academic knowledge. This has meant, principally, the mastering of the three "r's" in the early years with an upgraded curriculum to include history, science, social studies, psychology, sociology, higher mathematics, and so on as the child progressed to the upper grades.

However, more and more in our present age, the meaning of education and the responsibilities of the school are reverting, in many people's expectations, to the original meaning of the word, "to rear."

With the erosion of American family life, the increase in divorce, the accompanying increase in the one-parent home, the rise in the number of families in which both parents work, and many other factors, too many parents are taking less and less responsibility in the *rearing* of their children. As a result, too many of them are seeing their principal responsibility to their children as that of providing for their physical needs. Even in this area, an ever-increasing number each year look to the government for aid.

Even among those who still claim to accept the responsibility for child-rearing, a great number allow the time their family has together to be monopolized by the public media. The greatest problem we face for our families and our children is not based in the behavior evoked by television but in the behavior which television is destroying. So much in the home which was vital to child growth and development—long family talks, evenings of playing together, times of reading either with or to each other, the discussions and arguments and celebrations—are being forced out of existence by the television screen.

I agree with other educators that the television often transforms children, for the moment at least, into staring zombies who cannot be reached. I agree heartedly with the opinion that the *kind* of people they are becoming is left too much to the powerful influence, during too many of their waking hours, of irresponsible programming by people more interested in monetary gain than in building future citizens.

Thus the myth today is that public education should be responsible not only for the academic training of the child but also for all aspects of child rearing: the social behavior, morals, health habits, recreation, alcohol and drug orientation, the entire scope of child life.

I find the acceptance of this myth to be totally irresponsible and idiotic. How can the school which has the child only one-tenth of his time during the school years possibly be responsible for his *total* being. In my state we are required by law to provide 180 days of 6½ hours each for our school children. This is a total of 1170 hours out of the child's year of 8760 hours or less than 13½ percent of his time. By the time the child reaches the sixth grade, only 7 percent of his time has been spent in school. Who is responsible for the other 93 percent?

Of equal importance is the fact which a host of intelligent and responsible educators have been voicing for almost a whole generation, that the most important four or five years for learning and character building come before the child ever reaches the public schools. Among those who have called attention to this fact are Benjamin Bloom, James S. Coleman (of the famed Coleman report), Bruno Bettelheim, Jean Piaget, Ernest Q. Campbell, and Jerome Bruner. Typical of these is the statement of Don Dinkemeyer: "It seems pertinent to recognize that by the time the child enters school, a good part of his self-concept has already been formulated. Perhaps schools would do well to devote time to preschool parent education."

I am not sure that the public school rather than the community as a whole should be saddled with this responsibility. But the point is certainly well taken. The home is the ideal learning situation for the young child. His school teacher often sees the child for the first time when he comes in September (or later) and often does not ever see him again after he leaves in June. The teacher has one room filled with at least twenty-five children. She has, supposedly, six and one half hours with them. However, they are out to PE for thirty minutes, she takes them to lunch for thirty minutes, between rest, recess, and movements to and from these places she loses more than another thirty minutes. This leaves her less than five hours for a state prescribed curriculum. This curriculum concentrates on the basics and allows a minimum time for music, art, and practically none for teaching values and ethics, except as they can be worked into the other subjects.

The home, on the other hand, usually has a minimum of twelve years in which the child interacts with the same people. It has much more available space, has an average ratio of one adult to two and a half children during the day and better than that when both parents or a grandparent is present. In most home there is a wealth of materials for teaching math, social studies, health, and other subjects (measuring cups and spoons, yardsticks, thermometers, scales, to name a few). Children may be taken on numerous field trips without extensive planning: filling out forms, getting permission from families and school, securing extra transportation, and so on.

When voices first began to be raised forcefully about the importance of these early years, the federal government became interested and the Head Start program and the Early Childhood Project were begun. However, after a few years of energetic trial and error, they discovered they had put too little emphasis on the two most crucial elements, the parents and the home.

More and more research is now pointing to the fact that the ratio of success in improving the educational readiness of children five and under is in direct proportion to the extent the parents and the homes are involved. During this time, and *only* during this time, are the children influenced more by their home than they are by their peers.

Under a home-involvement program not only are the gains found to be higher but also they proved to be more sustained over a three- and four-year period. In most cases the greatest emphasis was placed on the child as an individual.

Benjamin Bloom, in his study *Stability and Change in Human Characteristics*[1] found much evidence that the difference in both the cognitive and academic development of the child can be traced to the value his parents place on education and to the amount of reenforcement in the home of the child's school activities.

He found that one-half of the intellectual differences existing in children of seventeen years of age could be seen in those children at the age of four.

A year later the Coleman report came out of Washington with the conclusion that the type of home a child comes from is much more predictive of his academic achievement than which school he attends or who his teacher happens to be.

The International Study of Educational Achievement in 1973 looked into nineteen countries and not only reemphasized these earlier findings on the importance of the home and parental involvement in the learning task but also went one step further. The conclusion was that the number of books and magazines in the home and the involvement of other members of the family in reading had a greater effect on the achievement of the child than either the income or educational level of the family.

Although it has now become general knowledge that parental aid and involvement is of utmost importance, this kind of assistance is not always easy to secure. I remember the first time this was brought home to me quite forcefully. It was the day the principal and I tried to send Timothy home for a three-day suspension. I had been working with him for several weeks and he was just one, big behavioral problem. At the time, our school was so full of such problems it was almost impossible to secure adequate testing and screening for them, especially on the lower elementary level.

Timothy would walk into the room in the morning, swinging his heavy overcoat, which was at least two sizes too large for him. He would swing it in a circle over his head just as fast as he could and would try to see how many children he could hit in the face or head before he reached the cloakroom in the back. He took particular delight in making strange, loud noises all day. Not only would he tear up his own paper if someone found he had made an error but if he realized that some other child had done better work than he had, he would tear up that child's paper also and then run to his desk and pull out all of the papers and books and scatter them on the floor.

On this particular day, Timothy had gotten angry with me because I had allowed another child to take our daily report to the office. Although he was a third-grader, he was as tall as I and quite strong. He picked up a metal chair, and with it held above his head, he began to chase me around the room. I sent for the principal who had already been informed about Timothy's previous infractions. He had warned Timothy repeatedly that he could not stay in school if that kind of behavior continued. On this day the principal decided it was time to suspend Timothy for three days. He was sent home, about a block away, with a note of explanation to his mother.

All was peaceful for about fifteen minutes. Then we heard her yell as she came through the door, dragging Timothy by the ear.

"Oh, no you don't! Not on my life you don't! You ain't gonna send this boy back to me! It's *your* turn to put up with him, and I ain't a gonna do it fer you! I keep him every evenin' and night and early mornin' an' I sure

THE MOST IMPORTANT TEACHERS

ain't gonna take your turn of keepin' him in the daytime. I'd be a stark ravin' maniac 'fore three o'clock ever got here!"

The principal tried to talk with her, but she was adamant.

"You's a man, you whup him! He ain't got no daddy and I'se so down in my back the doctor said I cain't fight with him no more. My brother was the onliest one could whup him but he had a heart attack last month and the doctor said he cain't do it no more. So, he's yore's, Brother! Take him and keep him and don't you ever send him back to me five minutes early!"

LaWanda's mother's situation was different, but her abdication of responsibility was just as complete. In her case, however, it didn't result in refusal to keep LaWanda, but in refusal to send her to school at all. The attendance worker and the social worker both brought back the same report. The house was full of young adults in their late twenties, and they greatly resented any intrusion or questions from any outsider. They were rude and evasive and both the workers were suspicious that the house might involve a prostitution ring. This suspicion seemed to be borne out by LaWanda's report of frequently being moved in the middle of the night and of a succession of men coming in and out all night. No one had enough evidence to bring a morals charge. However, as it turned out, that was not necessary.

After several attempts to get LaWanda back in school, I was watching the local news on television one night when they showed her mother and four other young adults being arrested for forging prescriptions on blanks stolen from a local hospital and attempting to secure hard drugs with them. It soon became evident that she simply did not care as much about her little daughter and her welfare as she did about trying to protect their operations from "nosey people snooping around."

Some of those who are slow to cooperate with the school seem to be overwhelmed with their load of work and child care and are afraid of being embarrassed by reports of their child's behavior. They come into a conference, painting just as bad a picture as possible of their child, seemingly feeling it will be less of an embarrassment if they profess prior knowledge and helplessness about anything you might be going to report.

I remember that Jocelyn's mother called out just as she was walking through the door:

"She's bad! I know she's bad! She don't do anything right. There ain't nothing you can *tell* me about that girl!"

My first reaction was that the only accurate statement was the last one, but I soon decided it was wrong too.

I did have some things to tell her about Jocelyn . . . . about a little girl who had such a poor self-concept that she began almost every sentence with, "I'm probably not right, but . . ."

Now it was easier to understand why. As you can imagine, Jocelyn desperately needed help but her mother was a long way from being ready to give her the kind she needed.

Some other parents try very hard to help their children but in a misguided way. Perhaps you remember Michael, whose mother was holding down three different jobs and his father, two. They considered they were "making all those sacrifices" out of love for their two sons, eight and eleven. And yet you remember Michael's talk of suicide and his pathetic question, "Who would care?"

Many other parents' reasons for noninvolvement are

not so dramatic as these, but the results are the same. Some are just too tired, too busy, or too involved in their own personal affairs and problems.

Every year during the last eight years, I have been able to get a number of parents involved in my own classroom. I think it has been a tremendous help to the children, as well as to the parents and me. I would like to see parents involved in our schools on a much larger scale.

However, I do not feel that all of the responsibility for bringing about this important involvement of the parents in the learning experiences of their children should rest entirely with the schools. It should be a matter of top priority with the whole community, especially with all of those intensely interested in developing the potential of our future citizens.

Throughout this discussion I have used the word *parent* in its plural form because I do feel that the most good in the life and development of our young can only come when it is a cooperative effort of both parents. Many contemporary women are taking issue with the old view of the male as an interested onlooker in the rearing of children. They argue that the fathers are just as capable and should share the responsibility.

In the November, 1977, issue of *Psychology Today*, Ross Parke and Douglas Sawin gave an interesting report called "Fathering: It's a Major Role." After convincing some reluctant postpartum personnel that young fathers should be allowed to handle their newborns instead of just admiring them through a glass window, Parke and Sawin completed a seven-year study of fathers and their parenting behaviors.

They began their study with a group of middle-class fathers who had all taken Lamaze courses with their wives and had been present in the delivery room when their infants were born. In order to avoid questions as to whether these fathers would behave differently than untrained, lower-class fathers, the researchers later took a group of eighty-two lower-class fathers who had had no training and observed them under similar conditions.

They did not find any difference between the classes observed, but they did observe that both the mothers and the fathers showed more interest in their infant when both of them were present.

Although half of the fathers interviewed in a follow-up study said they had never changed a diaper and 75 percent said they had no regular responsibility for the infant's care, other studies revealed that the fathers played with the babies more than the mothers and their interaction was a different sort from the mothers. The fathers would touch their infants with rhythmic tapping patterns more often than the mothers. The father-infant play would have rapid shifts from peaks of high infant attention and excitement to valleys of minimal attention. On the other hand, the mothers play was less tactile and more verbal and the shifts were much more gradual. The fathers would engage in physically arousing play and roughhousing. The mother's play was quieter like "peek-a-boo" and was more verbally stimulating.

The two observers concluded that the fathers and the mothers had different contributions to make, both of which were important. The father's greatest contribution to the infant's cognitive progress came through the quality of his play while the quality of the mother's verbal stimulations were the best predictor of the baby's cognitive level.

Reports of research from all over the world continue to bear out the fact that the best condition yet devised for the rearing of young children is in a family with two parents, where love reigns.

In an interview recorded in the *Nashville Banner* on January 31, 1975, Ernest Q. Campbell, dean of Vanderbilt's Graduate School and the codirector of the 1966 Coleman report, said, "It is important to remember that when we talk about school effects on learning we are not talking about the strongest effects." He went on to say that the major differences in scholastic achievement seem to be related to home environment rather than to anything the schools do.

The Joint Committee on Mental Health of Children put this very aptly in the following statement on the need for high priority of the involvement of the home in children's development:

All the world loves a baby. We as a society do not act that way. A newborn baby is a reaffirmation of the miracle of the creation of life. Most infants are near perfect at birth and possess enormous potentialities for bringing deep joy to themselves and others. They come into the world with great natural capacities for growth, for loving, for learning, for exploring and working. In them lies the hope of the future . . . for their families, their communities, the nation and the world. Our infants and children can and must contribute so much to these larger societies. They therefore are the responsibility not only of their families but of these same societies. We as parents and citizens must firmly dedicate ourselves to the members of our new generation and to fostering their maximum growth and development into happy children and young adults. We dedicate ourselves further to creating a society devoted to families so that, in turn, these families may provide the best possible primary care for their young.[2]

5
Doing Nothing Is Teaching Too

One beautiful, autumn afternoon I sensed that my first graders were loathe to stay inside. So I told them to get their pencils and sketch pads and we would go for a walk and see what we could find to draw.

As we cut across the athletic field, they were talking about the different shades of colors on the trees. They talked of different ways of trying to draw them and how to color them. Some of them began to wish they had brought their crayons along.

"Oh, the church! I'm going to draw the church!" Christy sang out as we came in view of the pretty church on the other side of the field.

"Can we go inside?" Ashley wanted to know.

"I expect it is locked up, and we really don't have much time if we are all going to take time to sketch," I reminded them.

"I've always wanted to see inside a church," Ashley persisted. "I have never been in one in my whole life."

"Me neither," said Anthony. "When my grandmother died they took her in a church but Mama wouldn't let me go."

"You haven't *ever* been in a church?" Helen asked incredulously. "Don't your folks believe in God?"

"I don't know," Ashley replied.

"I *guess* mine do," Anthony explained, "Cause last summer I asked my mama who taught the sunflowers to turn

DOING NOTHING IS TEACHING TOO 71

their heads all day so they was always facin' the sun, no matter what, and Mama said, 'I guess God did,' so she must believe in him, I guess. I never heard her talk about him any other time though."

"Did God make all the leaves turn all these lots of colors?" Alicia wanted to know.

"Of course he did, Dummy," Helen replied, somewhat exasperated.

"How do *you* know?" Alicia persisted.

"Aw, *everybody* knows that!" Helen answered with disdain. "Didn't your mama teach you nothin'?"

"I guess I just sorta figured it out for myself," Alicia answered softly.

When I heard her quiet reply I thought of the little blind Helen Keller who, when somebody told her about God for the first time, is reported to have replied, "Yes, I know him. I just didn't know his name."

As the children sat down to draw, I pondered on their conversation.

I thought to myself, This is not Japan where we were missionaries for sixteen years. This is Nashville, Tennessee, with its over seven hundred churches and yet there are children in my class who have never been inside a church and don't know whether their parents believe in God. I was thinking back to when my own five children were small and remembering how earnestly I prayed that one of the first five words they said would be either *God* or *Jesus*. I had a feeling that if this did not happen it would mean that I was talking more to them about other things than I was of the one I loved most. God answered those prayers just to reassure me, I suppose, for I realize now that the sounds "Ga" and "Jezu" are not normally among the first sounds children make. But everytime I would show them a beautiful flower, or the sun or moon, or rain or snow or a lake, I would whisper "God made it" to them.

Later that year we were getting ready for Christmas. I had told the children that we could write a play and make costumes and act out the story of the first Christmas if they liked. Some of the teachers told me I had better be careful . . . you know, church and state, and the ban on prayer in the schools, they reminded me.

"We don't do that sort of thing in schools much any more," one of them told me.

Something within me rebelled. Before I knew it I had replied, "One stinkin' atheist has intimidated my whole nation while I was gone. We taught the kids about the Pilgrims thanking God at the first Thanksgiving. That's history. I'm going to tell them this is history as Christians believe it. I'm not going to tell them *they* have got to believe it. Nobody fusses when I tell them about the Festival of the Dead as the Buddhists believe it when we have our Japanese unit."

Anyway, when we started reading the story next day, Nathaniel spoke up, "My mother doesn't know *that* story. I asked her to tell me the Christmas story last night and all she knows is *Rudolph the Red-nosed Reindeer,* and *Santa Mouse* and *The Night Before Christmas.*"

"Oh dear," I thought, "Maybe they don't want him to hear it. I'd better check."

"Nathaniel, what church or synagogue does your family go to?" I asked him.

"Oh, we don't go to any . . . ever," he replied.

I checked with his father.

"Oh," he said, "It's OK for him to be in the play. He's excited about it. Yes, my wife and I are Christians but we're going to wait and let Nathaniel make up his own

DOING NOTHING IS TEACHING TOO

mind. I just don't believe in teaching children anything about religion."

How foolish you are, I thought to myself. You are teaching him. You are teaching that it is of no importance to you. You have let him grow to be almost seven and you plan to let him go that much longer without once telling him what you believe or taking him inside a church. As far as his young mind is concerned, you are an atheist!

It is what I call teaching by default. It is the easiest kind of teaching. You just do nothing. I am amazed at how much of it goes on. If I lined up the children in my classroom everyday at noon and marched them to the lunchroom without giving them time to wash their hands, I would be teaching them that as far as I am concerned there is no need to wash your dirty hands before you eat. Some of their parents would be furious. But a large number of them do similar things every day.

Children are very alive, alert, little beings and are quick to draw their own conclusions. As long as you make a fuss about a lot of things . . . don't track in the mud, mop up the milk you spilled, clean up your room, comb your hair, hang up your clothes, and on and on, then when you don't make a fuss or don't mention certain things, they assume you do not care about them.

Let me just mention a few conversations in my classroom, and you will be able to draw your own conclusions.

> Carl: Can you watch anything you want to on television?
> David: Sure, unless someone else has to watch something else. Even then I can usually go and watch the little black and white in the bedroom.
> Carl: Don't your mom and dad care what you watch?

David: Naw, they don't care, especially if they are sleepy or busy. Just as long as I am quiet and don't bug *them*. That's all that matters.

Suzy: What restaurant do you like to eat at best?

Brock: Not any of 'em, Man, 'cept the hamburger places where you mostly eat outside and stuff.

Suzy: Don't you even like "The Fifth Quarter," or "Applegate's Landing?"

Brock: Naw.

Suzy: Why?

Brock: *Manners*! That's the only kind of place we ever have to have manners. I pass, Man. Mom doesn't care *how* we eat at home. We don't even eat at the table 'cept Thanksgivin' and Christmas an' like that. We can usually eat what we want wherever we want. That is . . . until we go to one of those fancy places where she's scared some of her friends will come in and see us. Man! If she's so worried, she ought to cue us in sometimes on what it is we are supposed to know.

Leroy: My mom doesn't care a bit if I get my lessons or not!

Jim: What makes you say that?

Leroy: Well, I get home and she says, "Hurry up and clean up. We gotta go get a hamburger and get to the bowling alley. I'm first up tonight." Then I say, "But Mama, I gotta get my lesson. You gotta listen to me read." She jus' says, "Maybe afterward. Hurry up, Leroy."

Jim: Well, does she let you do it when you get home?

Leroy: Naw. It's always too late. She's tired and I'm sleepy and I say, "I ain't got my lesson, Mama." An she jus' says, "That's the way the cookie crumbles!"

DOING NOTHING IS TEACHING TOO 75

Sometimes this teaching by default seems to grow out of inertia. The failure to praise is one of the things that causes children to feel you don't care. They draw a picture they are proud of and so they ask if they can take it home and give it to Mother. They write "To Mother. I love you, Jay" on the back of it. They get excited at the prospect of getting home with it.

The next day I ask them, "Did Mother like your picture?"

"Naw, she just said, 'M-m-m-m,' and went on watchin' her show."

It worries me sometimes that every year I seem to get fewer and fewer students who say thank you no matter what you do for them. When I make them cookies or cupcakes, unless I warn them in advance that I am expecting it, instead of gratitude I usually get:

"Can we have more?"

"Why is Suzy's bigger than mine?"

"Mine looks like its been cracked."

"Don't you ever make chocolate? It's better."

"If we don't like 'em can we throw 'em away?"

By the time I get around to all twenty-four of them, I've about made up my mind not to do anything like this again anytime soon.

I have a very definite feeling that one of our problems with our young people today is that they don't know how to wait for anything. They want everything now, or yesterday! The minute they get money they want to spend it, all of it. I took my eight-year-old grandson to the toy store. He had five dollars of his own. He refigured what he was going to buy about five times because every time he thought he about had his mind made up he would figure the cost and tax and find out he was still coming out with a few cents left every time. He was determined to spend all of it. He's fairly typical, I think.

Consequently, I work hard at trying to find some rewards with some delayed gratification built in so that the children in my classroom will learn that some things are worth waiting for. Over and over, I get the same remarks, "But Mother never makes me wait. Why do I have to wait?"

"Yeah, you can nearly always get what you want if you nag enough."

"Yeah, an' maybe cry a little. Sure."

Now, nobody has tried to teach these children that nothing is worth waiting for, but neither does anyone go to the trouble to encourage them to try it out—teaching by default.

All day long the TV trys to sell children on a sense of values that says what you want, what you must have to be happy, what all of their friends are going to have, is *things*. Things make you comfortable; things make you the envy of your neighbors; things are sure to make you socially acceptable; things will entertain you. Not many parents really believe or accept such a shallow sense of values, but they don't put forth the effort to let their children know that—teaching by default.

I admit that it is often the easy way out. Sometimes it is even a temptation in the classroom. It is easier to separate two children who are squabbling than it is to try to teach them how to get along. It is easier to send the very dependable half-dozen children on all the errands than it is to teach the others responsibility. It is easier to move the child who is falling behind to a lower group than to work during rest time and playtime to try to bring him back up to the present group. It is easier to call on the child who obviously knows the answer than it is to try to straighten out a wrong answer. And, if you do these easier things, what does the child learn? He learns that just a few dependable, quiet, smart people, who don't fuss, are important in our class. The rest, he assumes, are not of value and just have to be kept out of the way of the others—teaching by default.

Every year I get some parents who never seem to listen to their children. Children know when someone is not listening. It is just the same as being taught every day that you don't care or that they do not matter.

A lot of times I think of Angie and of the week she tried so very hard to tell her mother about our Japanese unit's open house. Every day she tried to tell her something new which we had made or learned or done. She told her each day when the day was coming, when she was to come and see everything and be served Japanese tea and rice cakes. And every day she would report back to me:

"I tried hard to tell her but she just won't listen. She don't care. When I get home she's talkin' on the telephone. When I go to bed she is talkin' on the telephone. When I get up and go to school she's talkin' on the telephone. I don't know if I can get her here or not."

When the big night came, I was waiting for Angie so I could help her dress in a kimono. She and her mother finally arrived. I struggled to keep from telling Angie's mother what I was thinking. The first thing she said was: "We almost didn't make it. I didn't know one thing about all this until dinner tonight. She said something about the telephone. Were you supposed to call me? Angie nearly dragged me down here. I wish she would tell me things before the very last minute."

After she had seen all of our exhibit, our Japanese writing, our haiku, our flags, our Japanese fingertip paintings, she heard Angie and some of the others sing two songs in Japanese. Her final remark was: "Why did you keep all of this a secret? I bet her grandma and some of the rest of the family would have liked to have come. I can't believe that Angie just didn't tell me a thing!"

Poor Angie. She looked at me knowingly and just shrugged. There was no way I could convince her that her work *did* matter to her mother or that her mother cares for her deeply.

Every year certain attitudes and facts turn up in my classroom that I am sure practically no parents would teach intentionally. Some of them have been taught by attempts to ignore them. Some have been taught by a look or an action. I'm sure some of the parents would be surprised their children had "learned" these at home. Here are a few of them.

- Sex is bad. It is never to be mentioned in polite company.
- Money is the highest value. It creates more work, more worry, more excitement than anything else.
- It is good to obey without ever asking any questions.
- Browsing and aimless reading just for fun is bad and a waste of valuable time.
- To just sit and think is bad. You must be busy.
- Cheating is clever. If you can beat a traffic light just as it turns red, or see where the traffic cop is parked and slow down just before you are caught, that's hilarious.

DOING NOTHING IS TEACHING TOO.

6
Scars Run Deep

The next problem I feel we should face is quite a contrast to the idea we have just left, that of teaching by default or doing too little. This problem, which might be referred to as the problem of doing too much, centers around the misjudgment and, often, the mistreatment of very crucial situations in the growth of children. The result is a personality which is so deeply scarred that it can only overcome the effects of the scarring by long years of gradually coming to grips with both the cause and effect of the mishandling of the problem.

It is an awesome thing to watch as a fellow human being and a friend peels back the layers of his innermost being, seeking for the answers that will tell him more clearly who he is and why some of his reactions seem to be almost beyond his control.

I went through this process over a period of years with David. I saw much of myself as we progressed but I don't think I have ever experienced a time quite so pivotal in my life as the one which stands out in David's early experiences. He had a deep experience of desertion and deception at the age of five. It affected his self-concept in a way that dominated long years to come.

His parents loved him in their own way. He was their only child and they were committed to him, albeit he grew up feeling he was a disappointment to them both. His mother had wanted a daughter intensely and had picked out a name for that dream child long before her pregnancy. She kept the name in her heart and mind for long years afterward in the hope that a grandchild would bear her chosen name and, in a sense, fulfill her unrealized dream. His father could not keep from making it clear over the years that, while he had wanted a son, David was hardly what he had had in mind. David was a quiet, sometimes sickly, pensive child with deep emotions, a love for classical music, and an interest in deeper, more philosophical readings than had ever appealed to his parents. His father had envisioned an outgoing, robust, hail-fellow-well-met, more like himself and admitted freely he had never understood his son.

However, although their intentions were doubtless good, they evidently made a very serious error concerning his upbringing when David was only five. He had been born with a stomach problem that would not allow him to eat many foods and left him with many digestive disturbances in his early childhood. A rather serious stomach operation which would leave him hospitalized for several weeks was decided upon as the only promising course of action. Whether it was entirely the decision of his parents or whether they had been ill-advised by one of the doctors involved, I am not sure. But it was decided that David would be told as little as possible about what he was facing. He would be left completely in the hands of the hospital staff. Presumably it was thought he would adjust better to the hospital conditions if he had very little contact with his parents and his home.

Without any kind of warning or prior explanation, not even so much as to allow him to see his bag being packed, one Sunday afternoon he was asked if he would like to go for a Sunday drive. Now in the mid-thirties that was considered a pleasant pastime, especially for a young child. He agreed eagerly that it would be fun and got into the automobile with great anticipation.

David says that he still remembers very vividly his sudden feelings of apprehension when his father turned down the familiar road that led to the hospital. It was his first evidence that this was something more than a pleasant afternoon drive. Almost before he knew what had happened he had been delivered into the hands of the hospital staff and was summarily left alone.

During the following days of pain, misery, questionings, and loneliness which accompanied the operation and the slow recovery he felt totally deserted, abandoned and, perhaps worst of all, tricked or deceived by those he had been led to believe he could count on. The depth of the scar this made on his ability to trust again is difficult to measure. To say the least, it took thirty or forty years to overcome it completely.

The hospital experience and the long, slow recovery was difficult. It included the task of starting to school when barely six on a strictly prescribed diet which he had to take to school in a jar, rather than in a lunch box with all of the tempting varieties of food the other children enjoyed.

He not only perceived himself as different from the other children, but somehow set apart from them. The betrayal involved in the hospitalization, along with his feeling of lack of support from his parents not only during that time but also in the general concept they had given him, that they were not pleased to have him as a son, left him feeling bereft and alone.

As he dug back into the memories of those days, David came to understand his rugged individualism that made him into such a I'll-do-it-all-by-myself person that it was hard for others to help him. The sense of desertion and aloneness from the days of early childhood, coupled with an adolesence which was filled with a lack of understanding of him as a human being, gave him the definite feeling that he was completely on his own. Sink or swim, it was up to him. He gradually built within himself a hard core of determination to be a self-made man, dependent on no one.

It is hard to say for sure, but it is very possible that this attitude may have been his salvation by helping him to refuse to give in to the lack of understanding and support he felt so keenly was engulfing him. On the other hand, this same attitude built a wall about him that others often found difficult to penetrate. It also gave him a strong sense of defensiveness. If he were a self-made man, then any criticism of him was felt to be a criticism of his core being. He was shorn of the normal trusting attitude of a child and thrown into a panic of distrust at an early age. This made it difficult for him even to trust God as he became a man.

It has been a long, painful road for David, learning to tear down his defenses, to admit that he does need people, and that he does need God. He has had to come to see that he is not, after all, a self-made man nor can he ever be. But there was a long process of peeling away the scar tissue around those early wounds before he could begin to be the self he was born to be.

These scars come in many forms. Often scars are produced by well-meaning but misguided people who think they want the best for others but they misread the other people when attempting to lend aid. Helpers often try to fit others into a particular mold. They try to fit them into their own idea instead of allowing them to be themselves.

I often think of Jim. Such an attitude on the part of his mother has caused Jim more than unhappiness and embarrassment. It has caused him to doubt the worth of his very being to such an extent I am not sure he will ever find real happiness.

Jim learned to read when he was only three. By the time he was old enough to go to school, he was deep into the fascinating world of books. That became his favorite pastime.

His mother's idea of masculinity was that to be virile and admirable, a man should be physically strong, an adept outdoorsman, and a competitive sportsman. She was unhappy and embarrassed by her son who cared little for this type of life. To her chagrin, he much preferred to be off in a room with a book than to be out in a neighborhood ball game.

She bought him expensive sports equipment and enrolled him in every activity she could find which she thought might help, from little league to summers on a ranch. When she realized that he was not going to change, she began to conclude that something was wrong with him. As she worried over it, she came to the conclusion that Jim was hiding behind the books. She tried to convince him that reading and literature were forms of escapism for him. She kept after him so strongly that she planted a seed of doubt in his own mind.

Jim began to think that maybe his mother was right. Maybe his disinterest in the rougher games of his friends had been a kind of fear that he would get hurt or that the games would show him up as inferior. Maybe he *had* sought to escape to his own room with a book.

The more he thought about her charges, the more guilty he felt when he tried to retreat to his long-cherished hobby of reading. He forced himself to cut back on his reading, but he was unable to find anything he enjoyed to replace it.

In it all, he lost not only the pleasure of reading but he also lost a lot of his self-confidence. He came to see himself as maladjusted and unacceptable to other people.

Perhaps one of the most common causes of scarring in young children is that which comes through divorce. It does not matter how amicably that parting of the ways is done. Nor does it matter how often the child sees the other parent. In almost all cases the child experiences a feeling of bereavement—a feeling of being left alone. Many children experience this as a feeling of being unloved and unlovable. Many also experience it as guilt since children are quick to feel responsibility for anything that goes wrong with those they love. Many studies have revealed that these unfortunate results are found most often in children who have experienced such a loss before the age of five or six.

I remember Eleanor. She was only two when her father left them. Unfortunately, the break was very complete. The father soon married again and had other children. He wanted to have nothing to do with anything or anyone that reminded him of his earlier experience.

Eleanor could not accept such complete rejection. Her whole life, from that point on, became a long series of attempts to win her father's love and acceptance. Continued failure and rejection over a long period of time left her an emotional cripple. As attempt after attempt to secure recognition and love from him ended in failure, she lost all faith in herself as a person capable of making such relationships. She felt unworthy of anyone's love.

At forty, she is like a small child in many ways. She

is on a continual search for love. When she decides upon a love object, she is content only as long as she is in the physical presence of that person. Her fear of rejection is so great that the moment she must leave the presence of that person, she is frantic to reestablish contact with a phone call or note to gain reassurance that she has not been abandoned or rejected. As a result, the normal human relationships that might help meet her deep needs are almost smothered by her constant need for validation.

Another friend of mine, Janice, was not physically separated from her father when she was growing up, but the psychological separation she felt was about as damaging. Her father was one of those people who always had to be right. There could never be another side to a question. He could not bear a suggestion that he was wrong. Out of his own neurotic need for acceptance, he often left those who loved him with feelings of rejection.

Janice grew up under this constant threat. She felt keenly her need of approval from him. She came to judge the rightness or wrongness of all her conduct by the extent he agreed with her actions. As a result, when her young husband abandoned her for another woman, she not only bore the loss, the hurt, and the rejection of that desertion but she also bore a great sense of personal guilt because she knew that her father saw all divorce as wrong.

After a long period of utter misery, Janice had the opportunity to pick up the pieces and love and be loved by another fine man. One great barrier stood in her way. She knew that her father's rigid code saw the remarriage of a divorced person as even more sinful than participation (even though innocently) in the divorce itself. Her own sense of values, her ability to make decisions, and consequently, her capacity for enduring relationships were all crippled by her intense need to find approval from her father.

The father is not always the source of the problem. It may be either parent or any person who is seen as very significant in the eyes of the child. In Maria's case, it was her mother. She was an emotionally unstable person who was in a constant state of conflict within herself. The victim of unsatisfying relationships in her own life, she constantly heaped her intense feelings on Maria.

All her life, Maria has had the feeling of being overwhelmed and unable to cope with the emotions of those around her. She is afraid of love. And yet she sees it as the ultimate goal for which she is constantly seeking. She is hungry for acceptance and validating relationships and yet finds herself following her mother's pattern of coming on so strongly that others back away from her. This intensifies her feeling of rejection on one hand and her feeling of being overpowered by emotions on the other. Although married for a number of years and the mother of two maturing daughters, she remains in an emotional turmoil that fears the thing she most desires.

I could go on, giving other examples, but I believe that these, along with others given earlier in the book, should be sufficient for my purpose. That purpose is certainly not to increase the feeling of guilt too often heaped upon the parents of disturbed children. No one person or one set of circumstances can be the whole cause for a child's pattern of behavior over a lifetime. One of the chief aims of this book on accountability is to stress the fact that all of us are responsible for all of our children. Every child whose eyes ever met my own, searching for approval or fearing condemnation, leaves me with an added responsibility.

I have given these examples of scarring for two principal reasons. First of all, I want to emphasize that these scars are often made at a very early stage and that they may have implications for the entire pattern of living. The second reason is the belief that it is entirely possible that some of the ill-effects and scarring caused by the inevitable, difficult times some of our children must experience may be tempered and even prevented by sufficient recognition of the problem the child faces and sufficient undergirding of that child by some significant other person in the child's life.

Although there has been so much written and taught over the last several decades about the great importance of the first five years of a child's life, I still run into many young parents who do not really accept this truth. Time and again I have had a young parent in for conference about the difficulties their child was experiencing. They have either disbelieved or chosen to ignore the warning. This has been particularly true of young mothers facing all the adjustments of divorce. When I have tried to alert them to potential scars in their children's lives, too many of them have replied, "Oh, she's still so young. We hope she will outlive it. After all, she may not even remember it, so I'm trying not to worry about that yet."

As I have sought for answers on what might be done to reenforce children during times of inevitable stress, I have been particularly interested in studies being made to determine the reason some children seem to flourish and develop without scars in very bad circumstances, up against incredible odds. These children have often been labeled the invulnerables. In a recent issue of *Psychology Today* Maya Pine gave a good report on this study of what she chose to label "The Superkids." [1]

In the last twenty years or so a considerable amount

of emphasis has been put on studying the risk factor in mental illness among young children, especially in the field of schizophrenia. The chance of the development of schizophrenia among the general population is 1 or 2 percent. However, in children with one schizophrenic parent, this rises to 12 or 14 percent. In the rare cases where both parents are schizophrenics, this incidence among the children rises to between 35 and 45 percent.

At least twenty risk research centers have been set up in the United States, Denmark, and Sweden. Six years ago these groups established the Risk Research Consortium so their findings might be better shared. Most of the studies have had to do with the pathology involved, but in the last three or four years they have become increasingly interested in those children who have *not* become ill and *why*. After all, if 12 percent of the children were developing the illness, that left the very large group in the remaining 88 percent who had managed to remain well in the same high-risk situations.

Of those children studied up to the present time, the well children have been found to have these five traits in common:

1. A social ease. They seemed to feel at ease with various types of people. They were not lacking in friends and always seemed to have at least one special friend with whom they shared many things.

2. The ability to attract and use the support of adults. They seem to have drawn encouragement from teachers, relatives, baby sitters who played key roles in their lives and helped make up for the lack of normal support.

3. Because they were forced to think for themselves and provide for many of their own needs, they reached a high degree of autonomy early in their lives. They often

created a little private place in an attic, a basement, a tree house, and so forth, where they could go to keep from being engulfed in their parent's illness. However, this detachment, if carried too far makes problems in forming other relationships later.

4. They seem to have a knack at controlling their environment to an unusual degree. They limited its influence on them by the ability to make much out of a very little. They did this so well that instead of feeling sorry for themselves they often thought of those who were still less fortunate than they and expressed a desire to be able to help them.

5. They were basically creative. Many of them were interested in art, music, writing, and creative hobbies. For example, one young boy turned his attic into a small model town in which he built houses, churches, schools, railroads, and so forth. Such children often scored quite high on creativity tests.

Others have listed the following three as characteristics which are shared by the invulnerables:

1. A good relationship with at least one other adult, especially during the first few years of life. This helped them to develop what is usually referred to as basic trust. Psychologist Burton White in *Psychology Today* says that the heart of competency in children lies in having another human being who cares for them in a special way.[2] He was willing to place a bet that no one would be able to find a competent child who did not have such a relationship. However, some researchers, especially James Anthony, have warned that too much attention was just as detrimental as too little.

2. Children need challenges to become invulnerable. Children who are overprotected, sheltered from risks

and difficulties, never learn how to meet such things head-on.

3. It is essential that the number of stresses a child is expected to handle at any one time be limited. Each added stress increases the intensity of the previous ones.

London child psychiatrist, Michael Rutter, identifies five risk factors in psychiatric disorders in children. He lists severe marital discord, low social status, overcrowding in the home, psychiatric disorders in the mother, and a criminal father.[3] He points out that a child with any one of these factors faces no more risk than a child with none of them. However, when any two of the factors are combined the risk factor goes up fourfold.

All of this research says that the early years in a child's life *are* of extreme importance in the formation of personality traits which will influence to a great degree his future happiness, competency, and self-concept. On the other hand, evidence is mounting that scarring during this period can be prevented or lessened in several ways:

1. By changing the environment through alerting those responsible for the environment to the potential effect it has on young lives.

2. By providing the child with a caring adult who will replace, to as great a degree as possible, the parent who for varied reasons is unable to meet his need for love and approval.

3. By providing the child with at least one person (whether an adult, a group, or another child) he can fully count on. When consistency and reliability are absent from the child's life, it is extremely difficult to build trust.

4. By providing the child an "escape hatch"—a place to get away from his tense living situation.

5. By providing activities that will allow the child to

SCARS RUN DEEP

succeed. In creative and satisfying activities the child may regain some of his sense of worth that he loses in the rejection he faces at home.

6. By providing opportunities for the child to grow. Allow him to be in on the decision making with regard to as many things which are offered him as possible. To be given some freedom to choose and to meet both challenging opportunities and discouraging prohibitions on his own will help the child feel that he *is* a controlling factor in his own little world.

In addition to these six actions, there is one other thing which all of us can do as our lives touch the lives of children. This was brought to my attention with renewed force when the young father of one of our fourth graders committed suicide. Jack was a top student and had a very close relationship with his father. Unfortunately, Jack was the one who found the body when he returned from school alone. Naturally, all of us were concerned about Jack and the effect of this tragedy on him.

In the weeks that followed, it was obvious that everyone was going out of their way to be considerate of Jack. He never lacked for encouragement, concern, and love.

This event caused me to change an idea I have had for a long time concerning relationships with adults to include children also. That idea is that we should treat every adult as if he carried some heavy burden because most do. This is truer for children than we often realize. The burden they carry may not be as traumatic as Jack's, but it is probably just as real and urgent to them. Their burden may be a rejection, a loss of love, or an impending failure. It may be a struggle with self-concept or an effort to transcend a very difficult home or school situation.

During the days following Jack's tragedy, I kept asking

myself, How different would this school be if we treated *all* of the children with the love and concern we offer to one whose problems and sorrows are evident to us?

We need to tread softly, speak gently, and offer very freely an encouraging and loving touch to all the children we meet. Growing up is never very easy. The love and encouragement we offer may make a tremendous difference in the number of permanent scars the child carries into adulthood.

7
Help Before They Start to School

Much is accomplished in the life of a child before he ever gets to school. He will have learned more in the first six years of life than he ever will learn in a six-year span again. He has learned to understand between twenty and forty thousand words. He has learned to speak three to six thousand words. As I pointed out in chapter three, his parents are the most important teachers he has had, or will *ever* have.

However, I hope that others besides parents will gain from this chapter. I will be speaking to parents, in the main. But, if a child needs to be prepared for school and will be a happier, more able participant for having learned the things and participated in the activities given here, then surely all who have a place in his preschool years—grandparents, relatives, church or school leaders, recreation leaders—will want to arrange their time of participation toward helping that child be better prepared for that very large step in his life when he enters school.

For a number of years, educators, child psychologists, and researchers have all known the importance of the preschool years in a child's education. By 1965, parents, politicians, and educators were all excited by the promises offered through the new Head Start program that was launched that year. It was to be a panacea for all our ills. It was to bring all the preschool children, by concentrated work with the disadvantaged, to a place of equal achievement and ability before they entered the first grade. However, even before it was well underway, rumors of a pessimistic nature began to appear in various literature. This continued until the final blow was struck by the Ohio State-Westinghouse Report. This report was based on a study of Head Start graduates. Although it was based on a limited analysis of short-term data, it was sufficient to destroy the public concept of this program as a panacea or cure-all. While Head Start has continued and grown and does a lot of good, it has not been a "cure" venture in compulsory education.

Many persons became involved in a search for another answer to the problem of the millions of children pouring into our first grades so ill prepared in the area of communications, verbal understanding, and basic concepts that they stood little chance of completing first-grade work in one year. They came to realize that one of the failures of Head Start was its lack of parental involvement.

Parental involvement soon became the new magic word. But we must not expect or promise it to be a magic formula, a cure-all. The first concept of parental involvement was that parents should remain in an advisory capacity. This was an improvement, but it left the parents in a passive role. They still were not directly involved in the education of their children. Such programs met with some success, but interest soon lagged. Parents were not deeply interested unless they could become active participants.

Other attempts were made at more active involvement of parents. However, this time it was seen as a need on the part of parents to be taught how to educate their children. Everything originated with the school system. Plans were handed down to the parents, and home visi-

HELP BEFORE THEY START TO SCHOOL

tors were sent to teach them how to use the material. This also met with minimal success.

Finally it became evident that the kind of parental involvement needed was that in which the parents and teachers worked side by side to supplement each other's work. Parents and others involved with the preschool child need to understand better what the school's goals and requirements are so that they can help prepare the child for the school experience. Schools need important informational input about the child which only parents can give.

Perhaps the greatest concern about our school systems today is the matter of teaching the children to read and to read well. Many people fail to realize that before a child learns to read he needs many things to help him develop the skills and understandings necessary for learning to read.

He needs, first of all, a basic, functional vocabulary. The size and availability of that vocabulary depends on his preschool experience. It is begun while the child is still in the cradle. It is important that adults talk to him and in front of him long before they can talk with him (when he can respond). It also is important that those adults who communicate with him use the speech of adults and give him as much information as he can handle. For example, a child who is just beginning to talk may see a flower and ask, "Wha-zat?" He may get one of five levels of answers:

"Fow-wer" (from those who try to answer in kind)
"Flower"
"A red flower"
"That's a red flower." (Hurrah! A whole sentence!)
"That's a red tulip. Isn't it a *pretty flower?"* It doesn't take much imagination to identify which answer will help

the child build an adequate vocabulary first.

So, first and foremost, a child needs to *hear* words. He should be talked to, played with (using speech, finger plays, nursery rhymes), sung to, and read to every day.

Every attempt the child makes to return the communication—a sigh, a smile, a coo, a sound—should be recognized and received as worthy. When the child begins to talk well enough to communicate ideas fairly well, usually about three years of age, it is a good idea to let him talk into a tape recorder. He will greatly enjoy hearing himself talk. The words can then be written down in print (manuscript) and read back to him. He will soon get the idea that books and stories are, as one small boy put it, "talk wrote down."

Some children are in school for several months before it finally dawns on them that those A B C's on the pages make words, and words make stories, and stories are for reading and listening to. Children who have been read to a lot, have watched the words on the pages, and have watched others in their home enjoying reading, quite often will be a big jump ahead of those less fortunate.

There are so many simple concepts taught in the first grade that many children come to school knowing and, therefore, are able to move rapidly to more advanced material. I am convinced more children would come with many of the concepts and skills already in hand if adults around them realized they needed them. Many of the things a child needs to know can be worked into the daily routine of the home or playground. Let me give you a few examples.

Sorting socks—When you are putting away the laundry, if you will allow the preschooler to sort such things as the socks, he will learn such vital ideas as matching, likes,

HELP BEFORE THEY START TO SCHOOL 97

unlikes, colors, little ones, big ones, large ones, small ones, larger than, smaller than, short, and long.

Making sandwiches—Count pieces of bread needed, help decide on the filling, square, four sides, triangle, three sides, spread from corner to corner, put spread on the bottom piece, put the other piece on top, whole one, half one, thick, thin, and a jar may be full, almost full, half full, or almost empty.

Pots and pans—Get out two pans with tops. Let the child match tops to pans, hand you the largest pan, smallest pan, the square pan, talk of differences, sides of pan, and bottom of pan. Discuss what you cook in pans. For example, let the child name all the vegetables he knows: peas, beans, potatoes, carrots, spinach, squash, and so forth.

Telling time—A child doesn't need to come to the first grade already telling time, but if you use the clock with him he learns what it is for and will gain some concepts and vocabulary that will help later. For example, when both hands are up at the top it is lunchtime. When both hands are at the bottom, it is dinner time. When we need to cook something ten minutes the big hand will move from here to here and the bell will ring so we will know to remove the pan from the heat or burner. Can you count to twelve? There are twelve hours on the clock. If you will tell me when the long hand is on the five and the short hand is at the top, we will watch *Sesame Street.*

Listening—This is very important. There are many games which can make the young child conscious of using his ears well. Blindfold one child and let him try to decide what makes a given noise, for example tearing paper, clapping hands, marching feet, running water, snapping fingers, coughing, something dropped on the floor, and so forth.

Another game is trying to decide which animal makes a given sound. Take turns making various animal sounds while the other one guesses which animal made the sound.

Still another listening, as well as imitating, sound game is to let a child be blindfolded or with back turned while you make a given number of beats or rhythm on a drum or a can and then let the child try to repeat the sound, such as dum, dum, dum, dum, DUM-dum-dum, DUM-dum-DUM-dum, dum-DUM-dum-DUM, and so on.

Use of the other senses—This may become games also. Feeling becomes a game when several objects are placed in a sack and the child is allowed to put his hand inside and try to identify the objects by touching and feeling alone. Put in such items as a pencil, a spoon, a spool, a cup, a small ball, a block, and so forth.

The sense of smell becomes a game when a blindfolded child is allowed to smell and try to identify several items such as a lemon, peppermint flavoring, perfume, coffee grounds, cold cream, onion, and so forth.

Both seeing and thinking are challenged when a child is allowed to see several objects on a table and, while he closes his eyes, one is removed. He then tries to remember and tell what is missing. A bit more complicated form of this is to place several sets of things that normally go together and let the child try to put them in matching pairs. Some pairs you might try are cup and saucer, shoe and sock, comb and brush, glove and mitten, pencil and paper, salt and pepper, and so on. It's fun, and it is a first step toward categorizing.

Other concepts the child needs to know and around which you can build games and activities are listed below.

Colors:
red, yellow, blue,
green, black, brown,
orange, purple

Shapes:
circle, rectangle, square,
triangle, diamond, oval

Animals:
Recognize and name pets, wild animals, zoo animals

Space and Size

up—down	large—small
in—out	fast—slow
top—bottom	wide—narrow
before—after	first—middle—last
above—below	big—little
under—over	tall—short
left—right	around—through
front—back	forward—backward—sideways

Parts of the body

head	knees	fingernails
toes	eyes	hips
hands	mouth	calf
arms	nose	waist
fingers	ears	neck
legs	ankle	thighs
tongue	wrist	eyelashes
teeth	lips	knuckles
elbow	shoulder	eyebrows

Things to ride in

cars	trucks	bus
automobile	taxi	train
airplane	helicopter	wagon
motorcycle	bicycle	sled

Articles of clothing

dress	shirt	blouse
pants	jacket	shorts
sweater	coat	gloves

mittens	raincoat	cap
hat	socks	shoes
scarf	handkerchief	skirt

Teaching children to differentiate between sounds is also very important. The listening games already mentioned are good starters. Beginning consonant sounds games can be started without even naming the letters involved. For example, think of all the boys' names that start like bat, ball, and bike (Bob, Bill, Brian, Bruce). Think of girls' names with the same beginning sound (Betty, Beth, Barbara, Belinda, Betsy). Think of boys' names that begin with the same sound as map, milk, mud, mop (Mark, Micky, Matthew, Michael, Marvin), or girls' names (Mary, Misty, Martha, Marian). Another form of this game can be played while riding in the car. Look for all the objects you can find that begin with a given letter. For example, instead of asking for words that start with a *D*, which you can do a little later, say something like "The key word is David. Find everything you can that begins like David as you ride along." (door, dentist, dairy, driveway, drive-in, doctor, dandelions, dogs, ducks, daisies, and so on.)

After the child has learned the alphabet it is a good idea to choose one letter at a time and look for it in signs as you drive along. Perhaps you will announce that today is *M* day and you will start looking for such signs as McDonald's, Milk, Moving van, Murphy's, and so forth. Later, when learning has become sophisticated enough to recognize *all* of the alphabet, let them play the old familiar alphabet game—front seat competes with the back seat (or left side with right side) in trying to find the entire alphabet in proper order on signs as you pass.

Other simple games or activities can be built around

counting and math concepts. For example, if a child can follow simple commands, try some like these: bring me five small blocks. Take two of them back. How many do I have left? Bring me three spoons. Now bring me three more. How many do I have in all? Bounce the ball five times. Can you jump the rope eight times? Carol has four marbles. How many would one more give her? You have four blocks. If I have one less than you, how many would I have?

Practice in the following of directions, first simple ones and then more complex ones is very important. "Bring me your plate" might be a simple starter. Add one more command each time and see how many the child can perform. For example, "Bring me your plate and put your fork and spoon in the sink." "Bring me your plate, put your fork and spoon in the sink, and throw away your paper napkin." "Bring me your plate, put your fork and spoon in the sink, throw away your paper napkin, and turn off the light."

For more sophisticated visual discrimination practice than in the simple "What is missing?" game above, take a pencil or crayon and draw a picture, not quite complete and let the child figure out what is missing. For example, a dog with only three legs, a face with one eye, a bird without a tail, a wagon without a tongue, a girl with both shoes but only one sock.

Take advantage of nature items outside your house. Look together for a spider web and explain how a spider spins the thread from a liquid which comes out of its body and hardens as soon as it hits the air. Help the child decide *why* the spider spins the web. Explain that only a few spiders are harmful. Most of them are helpful in that they catch harmful or pesky insects such as flies, fleas, and mosquitos.

Let your child help you grow something. A sweet potato plant is an easy choice. Cut the potato in half. Fill two jars with water and place the potato in the top or mouth of the jars. Explain the need to put the plant in a dark place for a few days. Let the child examine it once a day waiting for it to sprout. Explain that all plants need sunshine (set it in a window), water (keep the jar almost full), and food (the potato provides the food in this case). Explain that the hairy shoots appearing in the jar are roots. The sprouts in the air are becoming vines and leaves. Tell how a farmer plants potatoes in the soil. After they grow large enough he digs them, puts them in a basket, and takes them to market.

Talk of seasons with your child. We know it is autumn or fall because the leaves turn beautiful colors. It is getting cooler because winter is on the way and it will get much colder. We will have frost and ice and snow this winter. But when winter is over the leaves will grow back and the grass will turn green again. Lots of birds will return from the south and begin singing and the flowers will bloom. The days will be warm and that will be spring!

Take your child with you as often as you can to as many places as you can. Make each simple errand into an excursion or field trip. Make trips to the post office, the airport, the bus terminal, the hospital, and the grocery a chance to explain the services these places offer the community and the type of work people do there.

As you look back over these and other suggestions and wonder what *you* can do to give some preschooler some help toward a better academic education, remember that anytime you talk to him or take him some place or read to him or do anything to increase his vocabulary and understanding or broaden the scope of his knowledge, you have made a worthy contribution to his life.

8
So You Have a Child in Grade School!

Oftentimes, when I become overwhelmed in all the preparation necessary to get a year started off right—especially for first-graders—I remember Barbara Johns. The thrill in her voice, the joy in her eyes, keep me reminded that it is all worth the effort. The memory of it still gives me the same lift it did that morning several Septembers ago when she came bounding into my room exclaiming, "This is absolutely the most exciting day of my life! I've been waiting with bated breath for six years. That first day in the hospital when they brought John Paul to me for the very first time, I lay there looking at him and trying to imagine what this day would be like . . . my son starting to school! Oh, it's going to be a great day for John Paul and me."

I assured her. "I certainly hope it meets your pleasant expectations."

"Oh, it does, believe me!" she insisted. "You look just like I thought you would. The room is even better. I hadn't expected all the flowers and pictures and bright colors. I hadn't imagined it would be so inviting."

I could have hugged them both on the spot. Suddenly I wasn't tired, and all the effort seemed quite worthwhile.

It *is* a big day. And school days are happy, exciting days—days filled with wonder and enthusiasm and the desire to learn. To understand the extreme importance of these grade-school years we need to understand children from ages six to ten or eleven and some of the changes that are taking place in them and their world.

Up to this time, their world has centered around the immediate family. They have been quite dependent on their parents and have not had many interests outside the home environment. Now, they are entering into a period in which they will come to have a fuller concept of their own identity. They will become more conscious of their places as male or female. They will learn to enlarge the scope of their friendships and interests to include a larger community than their own home environment. More people and institutions and experiences will play a part in their socialization.

The early school years will be a time of growth and intellectual development. However, these years are sandwiched in between the two periods of extremely rapid growth, early childhood and adolescence. During these early school years growth slows down enough to provide a lot of energy for doing many things—playing, exploring, and practicing many physical skills—without experiencing any great fatigue.

Perhaps it is a time when parents know the least about their children. This is not surprising because, as many educationalists have pointed out, it is a time when the children deliberately turn away from the adults around them to become a part of the magical world about them, the world of children.

In this world, they have many things they share with great enthusiasm, whether they are appreciated by adults. For example, there are the endless jingles:

> Mary Mack, Mack, Mack,
> Dressed in black, black, black,
> Silver buttons, buttons, buttons
> Up 'n down her back, back, back.

There are jump-rope rhymes like:

> Cinderella, dressed in yellow
> Went upstairs to kiss her fellow.
> Made a mistake and kissed a snake;
> How many stitches did it take?
> One, two, three, four, and on and on

Or,

> Teddy bear, teddy bear
> Turn around.
> Teddy bear, teddy bear
> Touch the ground.
> Teddy bear, teddy bear,
> Tie your shoe.
> Teddy bear, teddy bear,
> Skadoo! Skadoo!

There are the ever-present jokes—the knock-knock jokes, the moron jokes, the elephant jokes. Their games have not varied much over the centuries: Hide and Seek, Tag, Leap Frog, Statues, Mother May I?, Red Light, Red Rover, Hop Scotch. They count out the way my great-grandmother did:

> One potato, two potato,
>   Three potato, four,
> Five potato, six potato,
>   Seven potato, more
> O-U-T spells out goes you,
> You old dirty dishrag *you!*

There are many rituals too. If you say the same word at the same time, you must lock little fingers and make a wish. If you see a thousand-legged worm, you must keep your lips closed tightly to keep your teeth from falling out! Be careful not to step on a crack or you'll break your mother's back!

As children enter this inviting world of middle childhood, their thoughts and actions center more and more around their peers and less and less around the adults in their lives. It is important to them to "be on the team," to enter into the same activities, dress the same, and act the same as the majority of the gang. There are always some leaders among the children who seem to have less trouble than others in breaking with home and moving confidently into this new world of peer-group centered activities. These children are greatly admired by the others. They long to be paired with them ("May *Joe* and I do it?" "May I sit with *Joe?*" "Joe is *my* partner.") They are pleased to find they have something like this child. ("Look, Teacher, look! My new shoes are just like Joe's!")

During the first two or three years of their entrance into this society of children, most children still have a strong desire to please adults. Because of this, praise becomes a very strong motivator. As children move on toward the second half of this period, especially from the sixth grade on, the group becomes more and more important and less conscious efforts are made to please adults. However, this is not to say that adults are not important to them. They desperately need the undergirding of their love and their votes of confidence.

As we take a look at what is happening in the lives of children during this period, one vivid way we can see and understand it is to look at what educational psychologists have called the developmental tasks of the period. The developmental tasks concept is one way of looking at the processes of growth that come in a lifetime. Life is divided into stages of development. The concept is that certain tasks must be accomplished at each stage on the road to maturity so that the tasks of the following stages may be built upon them. This is *not* to say that the tasks of any stage represent the curriculum for that age. They are, instead, an expression of the learning and behavior which must take place if the child is to move on into the next stage of growth and development.

Perhaps the most noted of those who seek to identify the developmental tasks of each stage of growth is Robert J. Havighurst.[1] He bases the growth tasks of the period of middle childhood in three great outward pushes:

The *social push,* which pushes the child from his world of home to a world of children and peer groups.

The *physical push,* which requires the acquisition of many skills in order to enter the world of competition and games.

The *intellectual push* toward the adult world of logic, symbols, concepts, and communication.

Havighurst's developmental tasks are based on these three essential thrusts in the growth of the child during this period. Those tasks, stated simply, are:

(1) The acquiring of physical skills needed for work and for games
(2) The building of wholesome attitudes toward oneself and one's growth
(3) The acquisition of social skills needed to get along with his peers
(4) The understanding of maleness and femaleness in our society
(5) The development of basic educational skills needed for reading, writing, and computation
(6) The comprehension of concepts needed in everyday living

(7) The moral development involved in conscience and a sense of values
(8) The achievement of relative independence on a personal level
(9) The development of acceptable attitudes toward social groups and institutions

As we look at these various aspects of development, we need to keep in mind that each child is unique and experiences growth at his own unique rate. To say that all eight-year-olds will act at a given level is not correct. Some will move faster and act more like the "average" (which is in itself a hypothetical misnomer) ten-year-old. Some other child may progress at a slower rate. This does *not* mean that he is inferior. It has to do with his nature, his environment, his experiences up to this point, and many other things.

Another thing we need to remember is that for any given child the rate of growth may vary greatly from time to time. Many children seem to grow by spurts, followed by fairly static periods. Also, many children are able to deal with some concepts more maturely than others. With this in mind, let us take a look at the three areas of growth mentioned previously.

The Physical Development—Two of the basic developmental tasks are tied to the child's physical development. These are (1) the acquiring of physical skills for games and for work and (2) the building of wholesome attitudes toward oneself and one's growth.

The rate of growth during this period is less rapid than during the preschool or the adolescent years. Girls usually shoot ahead of boys during this period and are often a year of more ahead in height and general body development. This sometimes makes it difficult to provide for

SO YOU HAVE A CHILD IN GRADE SCHOOL! 109

the needs of both sexes in a single group activity. But there also is a wide variation even within either sex group. One study of third graders, for example, showed a weight range from thirty-nine to one hundred forty pounds in a group of just over one thousand students.

Besides growth in height and weight, there are many other changes. Baby teeth are lost and new, larger permanent teeth sometimes look disproportionately large. Other facial features—the nose, the ears—grow near the adult size, sometimes before the head has grown enough to accommodate them gracefully. The lower jaw expands and takes away the childish look. Muscles are growing in breadth and width and strength. Boys are not yet stronger than girls since their muscular growth usually runs fairly parallel until puberty. Arms, legs, and trunk lengthen so that the child's proportions are more nearly that of an adult.

All of these changes, especially the rate of change as compared to that of his peers, has a considerable effect on the way the child perceives himself and his world. If the child is radically different from his peers, he is usually treated as different. For a boy to be short or puny or fat may be a disaster. For girls, being fat or not particularly pretty (such as having some feature temporarily out of proportion) or with hair too curly when long, straight hair is "in," also makes for problems. Children can be cruel in their honesty. They also are great label hangers: Fatso, Four-eyes, Shrimp, Lumpy. One way an adult sometimes can counteract negative labels is to beat them to the draw. I remember one little guy who was the smallest in his group but his dad, who worked with the neighborhood kids in ball games and such, had attached the name "Hot Stuff" to him. No one looked at his size as a disadvantage!

Adults who associate with children during this phase need to help them understand the changes that are taking place in their bodies and help them to realize that each stage is temporary. Children need help in learning to see the beautiful persons they are becoming. Poor posture, that may begin as an attempt to cover up height or early breast development, is harder to overcome than to prevent. Smaller boys need to recognize that size is not the equivalent or measure of success except in a few isolated sports such as basketball or horseracing.

Sex education often is a problem for adults during the time their children are beginning to develop. Adults need to realize that for the majority of children, sex education is a part of their growth during this period. Adults have little voice in the decision as to whether it takes place. They do have a decision as to whether they want to participate in the learning process.

Another thing adults need to realize is that sex education does not begin and end with the reproductive system. Of equal importance is the understanding of the male and female roles in society. Here again, the home is of utmost importance. If there is a power struggle with constant bickering in the home, the child may have a tendency to feel that sex, or living together with the opposite sex, is a distasteful problem to be solved or avoided. However, if the child grows up with adults who are confident, not defensive, in their sex roles, and who love rather than exploit each other, the child can deal with the whole subject with happy anticipation of adulthood.

We have spoken of the importance of the acquisition of new skills in the physical development of this age group. This acquisition depends largely on the motor development of the elementary aged child. This development will be marked by several changes:

SO YOU HAVE A CHILD IN GRADE SCHOOL!

(1) The change from general, overall activity to finer, refined movements. When a small child tries to hammer or saw, for example, his whole body is involved. A sixth- or seventh-grade child is more relaxed and performs much as would an adult.

(2) The change or refinement of motor activity usually improves from the head downward to the toes. Just as a very young child can hold its head in position before it can sit up, and can sit up before it can walk, so the older child can use the large muscles of the trunk and arms before he is able to use the smaller, more intricate, muscles needed in eye-hand coordination. He can throw a ball with fair accuracy before he can kick it with any like amount of accuracy.

(3) The movement of change, then, is toward a gradual refinement of eye-hand coordination and the performing of more intricate motor tasks. The first-grade child often has difficulty with large manuscript writing in block letter form. The third-grader, however, usually is ready to work with the smaller, more detailed forms of cursive writing. After another year or two, the same child often can assemble the most intricate model car or plane.

The development of motor skills involves three stages which overlap. The first is the learning stage. There are many activities a child wants to learn, and he learns a large part of them from other children. He learns to skate, to ride a bike, to climb a tree, to whistle, to wink, to spin a top, to play mumble-peg, to pump a swing, to swim, to play marbles, to catch a ball, to bat a ball, or to kick or pass a football. A girl learns many of these things along with jumping rope, playing jacks, or twirling a baton.

The second stage is the practicing stage. Children seem

to come equipped with infinite patience for this stage. It seems to me that I spend most of my playground hours at school counting for the children the number of times they can rotate the hula-hoop or jump the rope or catch the ball. I am well aware that our current champion for bouncing the ball has a record of 6,573 times! Finally, after the learning and endless practice, the child becomes skillful enough to put it all to use: Kyle becomes a track star; Paul becomes the home run king of the neighborhood; Helen wins a swim meet; our local tree climber is building a tree house.

Development of their motor skills is important to children. Those who develop a greater degree of proficiency most often are among the well-adjusted, popular, calmer, more resourceful, cooperative, and attentive members of the group.

In the earlier years of elementary school, children usually learn and practice these skills whether adult encouragement and supervision are available—if the child has a normal amount of time to play with other children. However, in the later years, children become busier, have more demands on their time, and are more conscious of their failure to compete well with their peers. During this time, children of both sexes need adult guidance and encouragement if they are to make hoped-for progress in these areas.

The Social Development—Social changes in the child of six to eleven are even more significant than the physical changes. Five of the developmental tasks referred to earlier fall within this area:

(1) Learning to get along with peers
(2) Understanding the masculine and feminine roles

(3) Moral development, including conscience and a sense of values
(4) Attaining personal independence
(5) Development of appropriate attitudes toward social groups and institutions

Growth in these areas will be marked by three changes in relationships:

(1) An increased independence from the family
(2) A pulling away from the opposite sex
(3) The forming of relationships with persons and groups of the same sex

These changes in relationships are brought about by internal changes in the child's way of thinking and feeling. Physical changes make the child more aware of himself. This brings a need to say, "This is *me!*" But this same development in the child causes parents and other adults to begin to see the child in a new light and to expect more of him. Adults may tend to do more structuring of activities for the child. The child, on the other hand, does not yet have enough self-confidence to deal with these expectations and activities without tension and anxiety. The child has arrived at a stage when he is more interested in his peers and their expectations. These two forces often cause the child to draw away from adults.

However, adults, and especially the parents, are of much more importance to the child at this time than the child realizes or would care to admit. The child is beginning to internalize some of the family values. If we could listen in on a group discussion when someone expresses a view contrary to these values, the child's defense of them might surprise us and convince us that he is more accepting than he realizes. While the child is fighting for acceptance and validation by his peers, the confidence that he has a place of acceptance and worth in his own home provides a tremendous buffer.

Some of the ways parents or other adults may provide this buffer are by increasing their sense of independence in the areas of decision making, entertaining guests, making future plans (such as for vacations and trips), arriving at and accepting responsibilities and, as far as possible, choosing their own clothes and their own friends.

Parents do well to provide equipment for developing motor skills and books, games, and music for intellectual development. However, the most important thing parents can do for their children is to make *themselves* available—available for talks, to answer questions, to help with special projects, and above all just to be parents when needed.

Helen Parkhurst, in *Exploring the Child's World*,[2] lists a number of rights that a group of school children identified in an interview as ones they considered important:

(1) To be an integral part of a family
(2) To be heard at times and about subjects which they consider important
(3) To have their opinions properly evaluated
(4) To explain
(5) To receive objective, fair, and patient treatment
(6) To ask questions
(7) To be given reasons
(8) To have a secret

If we wish our children to accept the principles of democracy, certainly we must acknowledge and award them such reasonable rights.

As I mentioned previously, along with increasing independence from the family comes greater dependence on the peer group. Two aspects of this dependence need to be examined: sex differentiation and the formation of same age, same sex groups.

Sex differentiation becomes noticable in about the second grade. First-grade children do not seem to have any great sex preference as to with whom they play or work. By the third grade, the division into groups by sex is fairly complete, but it reaches its peak usually in the fifth grade. This is not to say there is no communication between the two groups. There is teasing, chasing, running away, name calling, a bantering that seldom ceases. However, each is careful to keep their own group identity and would never admit to a preference for one from the other group.

Many of their preferences in games, interests, and entertainment reflect the group differences. For example, in listing favorite TV programs, girls chose love stories and family situation comedies; boys uniformly chose mysteries, horror, crime, and sports programs. Girls like kittens, fish, and horses. Boys prefer dogs, motorcycles, and cars.

Most educational psychologists refer to all of this as good. They insist that a child who has first learned to relate well to his own sex will relate better to the opposite sex later on.

These preferences for their own sex are obvious on most grade school playgrounds. Little groups of girls can be seen walking with their arms locked around one another. Boys usually are in another area in rough-and-tumble play such as wrestling, tag, or a ball game.

Both sexes like to form secret clubs with secret passwords and codes. Most of these clubs are short-lived and are reformed over and over. In fact, you sometimes get the feeling that the formation of them, the prohibition of the other sex, arriving at their secrets, naming their officers, and identifying their password is their principal activity. Once this is all accomplished, the interest wanes.

In these groups, however, children learn a lot of give-and-take, conformity to the group and its values, and abiding by group decisions. The group also provides much needed support for the child in this period of social growth.

The Intellectual Development—The intellectual growth of this age group seems to take on more importance and more problems with every passing day. Daily the children are having brought into their homes the problems of crime, war, government, marriage, divorce, unemployment, nuclear science, ecology, disease, and starvation. These problems are not from their own country alone but are pictured vividly from around the globe.

Children in this age bracket are said to spend at least one sixth of their waking hours in front of the TV. But at this age it is hard for them to divide fact from fantasy. And some of their make-believe horror shows are no worse than some newscasts. Children also are affected by the knowledge explosion. Some experts estimate that one-half of all present recorded knowledge has been accumulated in the last decade.

All of this has brought about a renewed emphasis on the three r's. Grades, test scores, and higher education all have increased in importance in the minds of parents. We will go into this problem much more fully later in this chapter as we discuss what parents can do to help the schools and, more specifically, their own children's development in the school.

The emotional development of children is dealt with throughout this book. The second chapter, on building

SO YOU HAVE A CHILD IN GRADE SCHOOL! 117

a positive self-concept, and the third chapter, on the need for love, are especially concerned with this developmental need. Another part of the emotional and intellectual growth of children is the spiritual growth and the formation of values. This is, in my mind, too important to be dealt with only as the final point in a study of development. I shall not attempt it here. Rather, I will go ahead with a discussion of parental involvement in our schools. Then I shall give an entire chapter to religious development and building a value system.

In no other section of our educational system are so many parents so deeply involved and making such a difference as in many American elementary schools.

From a teacher's standpoint, I had recognized the need for more parental involvement some years ago. I wanted to know more about what was being done already and how I might go about securing such involvement. I asked permission to do my Master of Education thesis on "Utilizing the Parent Potential in the Elementary School." The permission was granted and I found the research fascinating and helpful. I must admit that I was surprised, however, to find the extent to which some systems had been able to get many parents so deeply involved.

There are still some schools which do not welcome parents, even as visitors much less on a regular schedule within the classrooms. Of course, even in the schools that do welcome such involvement, there often remain a few teachers who consider their classrooms as their own private domain and do not welcome outsiders. Then there are other schools which welcome help in such areas as the clinic, the library, the mimeograph room, and, in some cases, the cafeteria but would not want them in the regular classroom.

However, many of the classrooms across the nation are

using parents as volunteer aids on a regular basis. Some of these come as little as one hour a week and some as often as several hours a day on three or more days a week.

Since attempting my first program of volunteer aids in my classroom nearly a decade ago, I have never had less than five parents involved and have had as many as nine working in one school term. All of these worked directly with students in the classroom. I have had others who were working at home to prepare materials, to grade papers, or to keep another mother's small child so she could work in our room. I have come to rely on their aid so much that it is hard for me to imagine a year without any mothers to help.

Do you remember my reference to Carla ("We's all bad.") and to Shelley ("My Mommie wouldn't take a hundred-million thousand dollars for me!") in the first chapter? The problem they presented is to me the most difficult problem to be faced in many elementary school classes. It is the problem of the extremely wide distance between the highest ranking and lowest ranking students in the class. With a ratio of twenty-five to one in a first-grade room (though I acknowledge gratefully this is better than many teachers face), I find it absolutely impossible to do justice to the totally unprepared children in one group and to the very intelligent, high achievers in another. I always have at least five learning groups and yet this number does not nearly meet all the needs of such a widely divergent class.

When our school systems have enough public support to either lower the teacher-pupil ratio further or to hire aids in each classroom to allow for more one-to-one instruction, then perhaps we can more nearly meet the needs of our students, especially in the first and second grades. Until that time I have found no method that compares to the use of parent volunteers in the classroom.

I have five learning blocks with five centers set up so that every child goes to every center every day. Of course some of these centers, such as art, creative writing, and learning games, have a wide choice of activities. The listening centers and the directed teaching of reading and math are more structured with fewer choices except in the varying range of difficulty.

Since I am involved in the teaching of reading and math to the various groups a good portion of the day, I would have a very difficult time if I did not have some parental supervision at the centers.

The volunteer aides make a tremendous contribution to our classroom day. Among such contributions are these:

(1) They help to see that such equipment as the Hoffman Reader, Singer tapes and filmstrip machines, the headsets, tape players, and recorders are used correctly at the various centers. This frees me from constant interruption in my teaching area by students who are having difficulties with some of the equipment at the other centers.

(2) They grade math workbooks and math sheets as they are finished, giving the children the advantage of immediate feedback and the pleasure of being able to chart their gain on the student progress charts right away.

(3) They make it possible to have many art projects which we would have to eliminate if we had less supervision. These include such things as block printing, spatter painting, working with fairly elaborate collages, weaving, making an eight-foot Indian tepee, writing Japanese *kanji* with ink, making signs, flags and fingertip painting during our Japanese unit.

(4) Much of the children's creative work can be displayed immediately by the mothers. If it were left entirely to me it would sometimes be a long wait since I am responsible for making all of the tapes and reenforcement activities for all of the centers.

(5) They can find more time for one-to-one interaction with the very low students and can give them praise and help in building the self-concepts they need so desperately.

When I first began, and even yet at times, other teachers raise the question of the wisdom of using parents in a room with their own children. When I send home my volunteer sign-up sheets in the fall I list many activities outside the classroom as well as the work inside them. These include such things as field trips, help with parties, occasional storytimes or music times, or such things as sharing interesting hobbies with us. I emphasize the fact that the principal and I always reserve the right to decide if it should ever become unwise in the child's development and best interest to have his mother present in the room. In these several years, working with sixty or seventy mothers, we have never had such a problem but one time and it was quickly resolved.

Many parents ask me, "How do I get my child in a classroom that allows such participation on my part?"

My answer is that it may not always be possible but I suspect a large number of classrooms do not have parent participation because they have never given it a try or possibly have not thought that they could get volunteer help that was so consistently available and cooperative. It would never hurt to have a talk with your child's teacher about the possibility. If she seems reluctant, perhaps you could offer to do outside-the-class things such

SO YOU HAVE A CHILD IN GRADE SCHOOL!

as grading papers, preparing art materials, cutting stencils, and so forth, which would, in turn, give the teacher more time for the needs of your child.

However, after having spent several years in the elementary classroom, I feel certain that if I were a parent of an elementary child again there are certain types of classrooms I would diligently seek to avoid for my child. Here are some of them:

(1) A sterile classroom, always neat, clean, free from clutter. There is no way that twenty-five active, enthusiastic first graders could work with any freedom in a classroom without making some mess and cluttering it up somewhat. None of our schools provide a classroom large enough to hold the many things in perfect order it takes to meet the sudden opportunities and interests of such a group. I admit that it would not have to be as messy and cluttered up as mine is much of the time but I would choose such a room far ahead of a sterile one.

(2) A classroom which does not welcome both visitors and aid from almost any reasonable source.

(3) A classroom that is consistently quiet and orderly. If I were to walk in on numerous occasions and find the children sitting in nice, quiet rows with little attempt on their part at interaction (which, let's face it, *is* noisy), I would begin to worry about my child. When children are interested, are helping each other, asking advice, and so forth, there will be some noise. I call it beautiful, happy, learning noise. When it begins to become destructive, time-wasting interferring noise it needs to be controlled. But unless there is a fair amount of pleasant interaction going on over a period of time, I would worry that the children did not feel the freedom and happiness that is characteristic of them.

(4) A classroom with too much detailed, determined scheduling which seeks to keep as many of the class as possible on the same page of the same workbook at the same time. I believe the years and the months, and even some weeks can be scheduled. But the moment-to-moment, day-to-day activities have to be flexible enough to allow for many changes of plans if the children's interest turns elsewhere, a rare mood needs capturing and capitalizing on, the children become so engrossed in an activity that it takes over, or the children beg to repeat it.

What then, *would* I look for in an elementary classroom? You can't have everything, as we all are aware, so I think I would settle for two qualities: (1) A classroom where love prevails, and (2) A classroom where creativity is valued and nurtured.

We have discussed the need for love in a child's life in chapter three. I think that love is contagious. Or in the words of a song the children in my room enjoy singing, "Love is a circle . . . the more you give, the more comes around." It is only where such a spirit prevails that the children can learn to trust and to be good friends that help to teach each other. They can often do for each other what I have failed to do alone.

As for creativity, I think too many people have confused ideas about it, two in particular. They see creativity, first of all, as a rare quality. I believe that all children are born with the urge toward creativity or they would never learn to crawl, stand, walk, or talk. I admit that this is overcome too soon in many people. If you will think for a moment of the accounts of stories of original sayings and creative play in children, you will realize that most of these are told about the very young, children three, four, or maybe five years old. But let these same children become nine or ten and no one is quoting them; no one is displaying their art work. Why?

In many cases there is now very little to tell or to show. Perhaps all of us have a certain part in the cause of it. Their peers tend to laugh at anything which does not conform. Too many adults have said to them, "Do it like I say and don't ask questions." Others who are not as authoritarian still tend to find creative children too messy and too time consuming. Most adults have become too practical and too literal to foster the imagination, pretense, and experimentation that goes with creative work or play.

Another misconception about creativity is that it is found in direct proportion to high mental achievement. In our schools, in those fortunate to have a program for the gifted or exceptional and creative children, the children are nearly always chosen for participation by their high I.Q. scores. This is a fallacy.

Dr. E. Paul Torrence, Director of the Bureau of Educational Research at the University of Georgia, for one, reports that 70 percent of the most creative children are *not* located through the intelligence tests. Creativity tests do not call for pat yes and no answers. They leave room for a child to raise questions, seek solutions other than those given, and to use his own ingenuity. A classroom should give these same options.

I know that these two standards are not too easy to find, but I believe they are worth looking for and worth working to help make possible. Evidently quite a large number of parents think so too.

9
You Have to Believe in Something!

I shall never forget a discussion I heard between two mountain boys when, as a college student, I was attempting to carry out a summer mission project in their small mountain community. I don't remember the name of the one who started the discussion with, "My pa don't believe in nuthin'."

But I remember Matt. He was the one who challenged him, "Yore pa don't believe in nuthin', you say?"

When the other boy insisted that was true, Matt gave the answer that stuck with me.

"That ain't possible. Believing in nuthin'—that's somethin', ain't it?"

I'm not sure how well, at nineteen, I helped to settle their argument. But I have been reminded many times over of Matt's answer. People who claim not to believe in anything believe that all of us who believe in something are wrong. They believe there is no God or eternal life. They believe the Bible is a book of lies. They believe that nothing in this great wonderful world is worth believing in. Every time I stop to think of it, I agree with Matt—that's something, all right. But it is a poor something on which to build your life and to which to trust your eternal destiny.

Nearly four decades ago, just about the time I graduated from college, Harper and Row published a book by Robbie Trent called *Your Child and God* that influ-

YOU HAVE TO BELIEVE IN SOMETHING! 125

enced my thinking for years. But one poem in that book, written by a little girl, has stayed with me verbatim:

I asked my mother what God was like.
She did not know.
I asked my teacher what God was like.
She did not know.
Then I asked my father, who knows more than anyone
Else in the whole world, what God was like.
He did not know.
I think if I had lived as long as
My mother, or my father,
I would know something about God.[1]

It is hard for me to imagine being brought up in a family without any teaching about God. I do not insist that all people must have exactly the same concept of God that I have. But I do insist that faith in God as Father, Creator, source of love and truth, with a purpose for every member of his creation is the only reliable center around which we can build our lives. It is the only center we have to offer to children around which to assimilate all we would have them learn so that they, too, may find purpose and truth and meaning and love.

I believe that teaching is sharing ourselves with the children so that they may come to love and trust us enough that, in return, we may see their true needs and help them in every way we can. There is no way I can share my true feelings on any one day, much less for a whole year, without expressing my feelings about God. I do not want any child to remember me as a first-grade teacher who did not consider belief in God was important. (And by not mentioning God I could easily teach that by default.) I try to be careful and make it clear that there are many varied ideas of God. I remind the children that many of their parents and some of their churches understand some things differently. Everyone must decide for himself someday what *he* believes about God. But I want the children to know that I feel it is important that they *do* decide someday, that they find something on which to build their lives that will give them direction and promise and peace and happiness. I do not use those words with them, but I do want them to know I believe with all my heart that God made them, that he loves them, that he is always near them, and that he has something for them to do that no one else in the whole world can do the way he planned they should do it.

I am amazed, in recent years, how little children have been taught of God. In my present class of twenty-five children, only one little white boy, Rob, and one little black boy, Daniel, seem to have been carefully taught. They are two of the most intelligent children in the room, so it may be that they have just asked more questions.

One afternoon a child asked that question, "What is God like?"

As usual, most of the children raised their hands to try for an answer.

"He's like a cloud," one volunteered.

"He's not like a cloud; he *lives* in a cloud," another corrected.

"He's an angel," insisted one.

"No, he's a king—the king of heaven," came the correction.

"Well, he can be an angel king," the other answered, willing to compromise.

"When my mother told me about him, I cried all night," Melissa said softly.

"Why was that, Melissa?" I ventured to ask.

"Well, we never had talked about him much but, when

YOU HAVE TO BELIEVE IN SOMETHING!

my father divorced us, my mother said I still had a father left. She said God is my heavenly Father. I cried and cried. I told her I don't want him for a father. I just want my daddy back."

After a moment of silence, Daniel spoke up. "I think he must be very nice and very smart. He made this whole, wonderful world."

Then Rob added his bit. "I know what he is like. He is like Jesus because Jesus said that is what he came down to earth for—to show us what his father was like. Jesus said that anybody who knew what he was like would know what God was like."

"Jesus was kind," another child added.

Encouraged by this addition, Rob continued. "Yeah, he made sick people well and blind people to see. He went home with bad people and taught 'em to be good. He even loved us enough to die on the cross to prove it. So that's what God is like."

I was very interested that, a few days later, when we were talking about wishes, these same two boys revealed some of the source of their concepts.

We first had talked of what the children would wish for if they knew for sure one wish would be granted. Then someone wanted to tell what he thought his daddy would ask for. We agreed to go around the circle once more and let every child tell what they thought their parents would wish for.

This time, Daniel and Ben were the first to volunteer. Once again, they gave thoughtful, serious answers. But only one other child followed suit. Cheryl said, "I think my mother would wish that not a one of her children would ever have to be sick or unhappy again."

Of the remaining twenty-two children, every single one was certain their parent's wish would be for material wealth. Two thought it would be for a thousand dollars. Practical-minded Eric insisted, "That wouldn't help much—after taxes. I'm sure mine would wish for a million dollars."

Cadillacs, an airplane, a new house, a big boat, lots of clothes, and a vacation in Hawaii all came in for their share of wishes. Most of the children were sure their parents would not want anything like the wishes expressed by Cheryl, Rob, and Daniel.

What did Daniel and Rob think their parents would wish for? Each of them spoke with a lot of confidence.

"I *know* what my mother would want," Daniel stated. "She would wish that some miracle would happen so that all the people in God's world would quit doing bad things and be the kind of people he wants them to be."

"It's sort of a hard question," Rob ventured. "I think they would have *two* wishes, but I'm pretty sure which one would be first with my mother. She would wish Jesus was alive again right here with us so we could know him better."

"And the other?" I asked.

"Well, they would wish we could somehow get enough money to send missionaries or someone to every person in the whole earth to tell them how much God loves them."

Small wonder, I thought to myself. Those two boys have a pretty clear concept of God.

Faith is very easy for a child. He is, by nature, trusting. Faith is an attitude of mind. Dr. David Seaburg, the famed clinical psychologist, once said of the mentally ill he has treated, "I have never been able to bring a man back to sanity and right thinking until I have brought him first to faith in God."

Robbie Trent, in the book *Your Child and God* mentioned earlier says, "This business of living has at least one resemblance to playing a phonograph record. To be balanced, it must be played on center. . . . I tried [playing it off-center] once when I was a child and I have not yet forgotten the utter discord and jumble of unpleasant sounds that came forth. Why was there no harmony? Because there was no balance to the record. It was meant to be played on center. Faith in God gives the individual a stable center, a permanent sense of security that colors his entire outlook . . . . It means ease of movement in spiritual imaginings. It means basic trust which enables an individual to move out into the sunlight of creative faith.[2]

Some people argue against teaching little children about God. One thing is basically wrong with this advice. It ignores one simple fact: The child is constantly experiencing God. He lives in a universe that is orderly to the extent it operates according to the laws of God. His body operates on the principles of the God who created it. He breathes the air and eats the food and enjoys the beauty of wonders of nature which God created for him. The slightest suggestion helps him to connect all of this with God.

No parent needs to ask the question, Shall I teach my child of God? It is a choice you are already making by your attitudes and conduct—positive or negative. Either you are teaching that God is important or that God doesn't count.

My feeling that teachers also cannot remain neutral on the matter of faith and values was expressed by Dr. William Davis, Ontario's Minister of Education, at the Fourth International Curriculum Conference in a report published by the National Education Association. He said, "It has been suggested that the school stay clear of value questions. I consider this to be completely impossible, not only in practice, but also in theory. Not only will a teacher be unable to keep his own views from a class with whom he is associated for a whole year, but a position of value neutrality is itself a value position."

When I read these words, I wanted to say, "Yea, Matt!" remembering the wisdom of my little friend in the Ozarks.

There are many varied concepts and definitions of values. After comparing quite a number of the most accepted definitions, I found three elements that were included in most of them. In terms of those elements, a good definition would be: A value is a belief which (1) is chosen from a number of alternatives, (2) is acted upon, and (3) which enhances creative integration and development of human personality.

We need to elaborate on each of these elements.

First, a value is something that is chosen. It is an integral part of the idea of discovery, formation, and identity of the person doing the choosing, at whatever level that person happens to be. It is a matter of seeing several options and making a deliberate choice.

In training young children, whether in the home, school, church, or community, this is a basic initial step. The child must be given enough options to learn to make choices. Unless the ability to reach decisions on his own is developed, later on in life he will have great trouble making decisions. Although he is old enough and has been taught to understand the options of right and wrong behavior, he may often allow others—the gang, clever advertisers, or a wayward friend—to make his decisions for him.

An example of allowing for options and decision making occurred in my classroom this week. Orville kept disturb-

YOU HAVE TO BELIEVE IN SOMETHING! 131

ing our math group and I was tempted to say, "Orville, come take this note and go to the principal's office right this minute to receive the spanking you need!"

Instead, in an attempt to let him help make the decision, I said, "Orville, I cannot let you disturb the group like this. You have three choices: (1) You may come and quietly join the group and disturb us no more, (2) you may go to the principal's office for a spanking, or (3) you may leave the group and quietly go do something else and stay in the room during recess to work on your math."

He thought a minute and decided he preferred to stay and be quiet. Being allowed to help in the decision making not only secured more cooperation but it also prepared him to participate in this first step in value making—choosing.

The second step in value formation is to act upon the value chosen. Without action the choice is sterile. To choose to do something is one thing, but to act upon that decision or choice often is quite different. Real belief is, in essence, a premise on which one is willing to wager his way of life. If there is a disparity between what is professed (the verbal choice) and actual behavior, one of two explanations applies: (1) I don't act as I say, or (2) I don't say as I do. To be a real value a person owns, he must act upon it.

The third element of a true value is that it enhances creative integration and the development of human personality. Some refer to this as the prizing and cherishing of the value, or the original choice. It is really a part of the second step—the behavioral extension of the choice—but it is more. It is coming face to face with reality and our limitations and being committed to act upon the choice over and over from now on.

Of course, in the young child these three steps are

simplified, but they are present just the same. The child must choose from alternatives, act upon the choice, and be confident that he has chosen the best life-style.

Most students of values and how they are formed agree that there are two primary values which, ideally, are chosen in childhood. However, if the adoption or integration of these values does not come in childhood, if they are blocked or thwarted by negative experiences, someone must help the adolescent or adult go back and deal with the difficulties and develop them before other values can be accepted. The first of these primary or basic values is self-value or the intrinsic knowledge that I am of worth to others. The second is the value of others.

If these two values are so important that all others must be built upon them, it is very important that a child should have a loving and caring environment in which to develop. For basic trust is essential to the development of these primary values. Self-worth, for example, is defined as a conviction that if other people really knew me they would believe me to be a person of value. However, if basic trust is not present, a child will not believe people even if they say he is a person of worth.

Basic trust is not destroyed just by deception, desertion, and lying to a child. It also is broken down by expecting more of the child than he can deliver. On the other hand, it also is broken down by expecting so little that the child is led to believe he has little value in the eyes of others.

As we have discussed earlier, meeting the basic needs of the very young child for food, comfort, and love is the thing out of which this basic trust normally is formed. Self-value comes when a child can see that his feelings, his ideas, his body, and what he does all are of value to himself and to others.

The second primary value sees others as also being

of great value. The child sees that if he is really of value, then others about him who are so much like himself must be of like value. The *self*-affirmation always must come before this *other*-affirmation is possible.

This value is not an unconditional acceptance of all a person *does*, but of what that person *is*. Love separates behavior from the intrinsic value of a person.

The elementary school, as the primary societal experience of the child away from the home, should help children learn to live and work together. In other words, this is a primary training ground for citizenship. This citizenship training does not necessarily happen during a special time set aside for social studies. The entire school experience, including what happens on the way to and from the school building and the way the family responds toward events related to the school, is the training the child receives in citizenship. Physical education, dramatics, music activities, school clubs, and similar activities can teach cooperation, the need for rules and the need to respect such rules, appreciation for the knowledge and skills of other people, the need for leadership (and "followship") and many similar lessons in living together.

Children need to develop an understanding and appreciation of those human values and disciplines that are a part of our democratic society. These human values and disciplines are expressed in many common phrases that sometimes are poorly defined. Some of these phrases are: being a decent, law-abiding citizen; being a good sport; having a sense of honor; not letting the other fellow down; taking turns; having a sense of fair play; respecting the rights of others; doing your part; being a member of the team; doing an honest day's work for an honest day's pay. Values and disciplines such as these can be learned through experiences in the school (and at home), and often they may be interpreted as individual experiences are discussed.

Let's think about how children learn to take turns. Many children enter school without a clear understanding of the necessity for this discipline. They always want to be first. They may experience repeated disappointment, engage in verbal or physical shoving matches, or find themselves rejected by most of the group before taking turns is accepted as a necessary part of living with other people.

At first a child may learn to take turns only when the teacher is present and gives direct supervision. But he must also learn to take turns when the teacher leaves the room. Then he must learn to use this process on the playground, during after-school games, at Sunday School, in the Scout troop, and in his home. The basic value or discipline may be learned or strongly reinforced in the schoolroom, but learning is not complete until it is applied appropriately in every area of life. And the child may have a difficult time learning this concept if the home, or another important influence in his life, fails to consistently uphold and reinforce that idea. When all persons who influence the child teach the same concept, learning is made easier for the child.

I have tried to point out that, no matter how we all try to build these values, it is useless unless the first two basic values have been firmly entrenched. It is well to emphasize that this also is true of those who seek to lead children. One of the most discouraging obstacles to come up against in trying to train a child is to find that a parent, or teacher, or some other significant adult in the child's life, has not yet integrated these first two basic values of being able to love themselves and others.

YOU HAVE TO BELIEVE IN SOMETHING!

Dorothy Law Nolte said it very well in her philosophical poem "Children Learn What They Live" (The American Institute of Family Relations, 5287 Sunset Blvd., Los Angeles, Calif.).

Children Learn What They Live

If a child lives with *criticism,* he learns to *condemn*...

If a child lives with *hostility,* he learns to *fight*...

If a child lives with *fear,* he learns to be *apprehensive*...

If a child lives with *pity,* he learns to *feel sorry for himself*...

If a child lives with *ridicule,* he learns to be *shy*...

If a child lives with *jealousy,* he learns what *envy* is...

If a child lives with *shame,* he learns to feel *guilty*...

If a child lives with *encouragement,* he learns to be *confident*...

If a child lives with *tolerance,* he learns to be *patient*...

If a child lives with *praise,* he learns to be *appreciative*...

If a child lives with *acceptance,* he learns to *love*...

If a child lives with *approval,* he learns to like *himself*...

If a child lives with *recognition,* he learns that *it is good to have a goal*...

If a child lives with *sharing,* he learns about *generosity*...

If a child lives with *honesty* and *fairness,* he learns what *truth* and *justice* are...

If a child lives with *security,* he learns to have *faith in himself and in those about him*...

If a child lives with *friendliness,* he learns that *the world is a nice place in which to live . . .*

If you live with *serenity,* your child will *live with peace of mind . . . .*

10
Seeing Them Through to Maturity

I do not feel that we should leave a discussion of leading and teaching children without discussing seeing them through to maturity. This involves a discussion of adolescence, the last stage they must go through before they can reach maturity.

I am bothered that so many parents and teachers tend to look at this period of development as something "to be put up with," a stage to try to endure, to hope to live through.

Actually, it is a fascinating time of rapid growth and change. It is a time when the need for patience and understanding is very critical. The adolescent usually does not understand himself and often is quite impatient with much that is happening to him. If he finds lack of understanding in those around him, the situation worsens and becomes more difficult to bear.

Naturally he is insecure. He is faced with some of life's most serious problems: his career, his place in the world, his selection of a mate, his ability to make decisions and act independently, and forming his own philosophy of life.

The ways this insecurity is expressed often puts up barriers for parents and others unless they are very careful. For example, the adolescent may respond with loud boisterousness one moment and quiet self-conscious withdrawal the next. His clothes and his grooming may be faddish and sophisticated while his speech is filled with adolescent jargon.

He complains about being treated like a child while acting very childishly. Adults who work with him must remember that, although his actions don't always show it, his greatest desire is to be an adult. He is trying to go both directions at the same time—dependence and independence.

A central principle of child rearing (for all concerned in it—parents, teachers, and friends) is that it should be a gradual shifting of control from without to within. Adolescence should be the final stage. Those who are going through it need our moral support. They need to know that we are on their side.

While the most common definition of adolescence, "growing into maturity," is very true in the broad sense, this transition from child to adult still must be viewed from at least three perspectives to be understood—the biological, the psychological, and the cultural.

First of all, the biological has the clearest lines of division because the body changes are obvious. Adolescence is the time when growth is faster than at any other time except the second year of life. With growth comes a sense of power. When the individual who has always looked up (literally if not figuratively) to the adults around him suddenly can look them in the eye, this gives him a feeling of equality he hasn't known before. It is not surprising that he soon demands that his new equality be recognized by the adults around him. Another aspect of this physical or biological growth is the sexual maturation that takes place. The adolescent may become greatly concerned about the rate of his growth—or lack of it—both physically and sexually, as compared to that of his peers.

SEEING THEM THROUGH TO MATURITY

The psychological changes which take place are partly due to the biological changes with the new stresses and responsibilities they bring. However, they also are due to the maturation of the thought process. This becomes more subjective—with a new sense of 'I-ness." There is a new autonomy in decision making. While the adolescent still requires some guidance to make mature, dependable decisions, he likes to *feel* like the decisions are his. And if allowed to make decisions—with some check by a concerned adult—he will soon be able to make decisions alone.

Another strong element in the psychological development is the change in role with parents. As mentioned, adolescents want to be treated as equals. Too often, however, they want equality without responsibility. They want the independence and joy of adulthood while the parents still bear the burdens. As one young girl I know expressed it, "I wish I could just be forever sixteen!"

The cultural aspects of adolescence have a definite effect on reactions to the biological as well as to the psychological. The culture in which the adolescent finds himself has a lot to do with determining the length of the period as well as how adequately the adolescent has been prepared for all that he must face. Far too frequently this preparation is sadly lacking. This means the youth is caught off guard and his sense of ambiguity is thus greatly increased. It should be noted that the cultural structures provide the context for the bio-psychological transitions of this period. It is, as Erikson pointed out, almost as if the adolescents have been given a "moratorium on growing up," a time of suspended responsibility to provide a time of apprenticeship to adulthood.

All aspects of this transition to maturity vary greatly

as to when—if ever—they are accomplished in any given individual. This is especially true in the area of psychological development.

Many things in our culture have had a definite effect on the period of adjustment and changes we call adolescence. In America, especially, this adolescent period is affected by: (1) the length of the period imposed by our laws and customs; (2) the prolonged period of dependency because of our encouragement toward advanced education, later marriage; specialized training for employment, and so forth; (3) the ambiguity of status as older adolescents *feel* like adults, *vote* like adults, *fight* as adults, and yet are dependent on their parents financially; (4) the complexity of our society that offers them so many alternatives—more alternatives than universals—all to be met at a time of great vulnerability; (5) rapid change which is hard on all humanity (for we all seek permanence at some level) but is especially hard on adolescents who already are having to face so much change within themselves, and finally (6) a delay in employment which touches on the need of all human beings to feel that they have a significant role in a significant world.

In all of my reading and thinking, I have not come upon a better presentation of the most important developmental tasks which all human beings face than the one given by Dr. William Penrod in a graduate course on adolescent psychology. It summed up all of the tasks of the search for identity and a place in the world in one encompassing phrase: "Becoming a center of freedom and love."

1. *Becoming*—This emphasizes that humanity is never static. We are always, constantly moving. Too often the adolescent overlooks the possibility of change and sees the conflicts and characteristics of his time as permanent.

Adolescents need some affirming, confirming adults to validate them, to assure them that change can and will come. They also need adults as models. They need constructive conflict with adults—to help them to establish limits and as an opportunity to throw everything out and examine it and sort it out. An adolescent bases his life on hope, trust, and for this reason, he needs the reassurance of validation.

2. *Center*—At any level of life there is some nucleus around which life is organized. (I like Dr. Penrod's example of the stack pole in the haystack.) We all need to be centered (not ec/centric). To be centered is to have a basic integrity, a oneness; to have developed a set or hierarchy of values. Some basic ingredients that create a centeredness or unity are: (1) decisiveness (or away from schism or split) to reduce the split or ambivalence; (2) self-definition—what we are and why we are here; and (3) commitment or faith. It is part of the nature of all humanity to want to know real purpose in life and to seek permanence beyond this life. The last basic ingredient is sexual definition—a need to experience self as masculine or feminine.

3. *Freedom*—Freedom can be defined as the ability to affect consequences, to be free from entanglements and distortions so that one may move toward goals which have been self-chosen. This freedom, as it is attained, makes possible the reconstruction of parental ties by getting rid of the residue of old conflicts. Freedom comes as the individual is able to accept responsibility. We cannot be free until we can say, "I did it. I am responsible." Freedom also encompasses the ability to synthesize the ideal and the real without being disintegrated.

4. *Love*—This does not refer to mere chemistry. It does involve a whole philosophy of sexuality. To reach this

goal one must learn to be intimate. This is difficult, because intimacy makes one vulnerable. This love must also include mutual respect, sharing, and responsibility. The primary motivation must become to give rather than to receive.

As I pointed out previously, these are the developmental tasks of all human beings. The extent to which they are accomplished at any given stage of life is relative. They are still a good measuring stick for maturity, even though they are lifelong tasks which will never be completely accomplished.

Physical changes that occur during puberty and early adolescence are very important because they become the symbol of all the other changes. All of our lives we build a body image. But the body image of the early adolescent, since it is the base of all operations with the rest of the world, becomes confused in his mind with his whole self-concept. If his body image is acceptable or unacceptable, he considers it a judgement on his total self. These changes are also important because they are so radical, so rapid. There is a new introspection, a subjectiveness, an awareness of self. He is constantly looking into mirrors, or spends hours on the phone with peers, seeking feedback on self. There is a great emphasis on peer values and opinions. Our culture, with its emphasis on the beautiful and good, has a great effect on adolescents as they evaluate their bodies, and hence their totality, and see themselves as very small when humiliated and "ten feet tall" when happy.

One problem that often arises is that of asynchrony or out of timeness. There is often a discrepancy between physical and sexual maturation or between physical and psychological maturation. There is always a difference in those who mature early and late which often affects their personalities and self-images. The early maturers among the boys usually have a positive self-image, are popular, objective, and sometimes over-control their feelings, probably in an attempt to live up to their he-man images. The late maturers often have a negative self-image, perceive of their parents as more controlling and show more nervousness. However, they often tolerate ambiguity better, are more flexible, and have a better sense of humor.

Girls often cannot handle themselves as well if there is too much incongruity between their physical and psychological development. Perhaps this is because their physical development (or lack of it) is so obvious that, regardless of their own thoughts and feelings, they are treated accordingly. The girl who looks sexually mature is often treated as more mature than her underdeveloped peers. The girl who is slow to develop, on the other hand, is often still treated like a child.

Perhaps more should be said here about the nature and function of the sex-role identity in the personality development of the adolescent. One's sex is one of the most powerful single determinants of how we are treated from birth. A different set of behaviors and expectations are applied to a male or female child.

There is a set of inherent qualities which we have labeled masculine. This is not to say "male" or "female," but qualities found more prominently in the male. Among these traits are aggressive, dominant, independent, analytical, intellectual, abstract, master of his environment, rational (non-affective), powerful, expecting obedience, rigid, quantitative.

Another set of inherent qualities, we label as feminine. Among these are dependence, submission, artistic, creative, concrete (in the sense of immediate atunement to experience), receptive, affective, personally related, peaceful, loving, qualitative, holistic, and nurturent.

These two sets of qualities correspond roughly to those people who are right-brain oriented (feminine) and left-brain hemisphere oriented (masculine). The problem in all of this is that too many people have a stereotyped idea that males should all have masculine qualities and females should all have feminine qualities. Actually, all people are a combination of the two. More males are predominantly masculine and more females are predominantly feminine.

In defining sex-roles, we must consider three different viewpoints:

(1) *Sex-role orientation.* This is a person's subjective evaluation of his own self, how he conceives himself to be.

(2) *Sex-role preference.* This refers to the feminine and masculine values listed above and the individual's preference or integration of these characteristics.

(3) *Sex-role adoption.* This is the role which the individual takes over either from a model or from the feedback he receives from others (that is to say, "He is such a sissy" or "She's a tomboy") and correlates it into his own behavior.

Some males (such as a large number of blacks who have never known a father figure) who do not have a male to identify with and feel deprived of their sex-role, come to overemphasize their maleness by running with rough, dominating street gangs.

We must give some attention to family constellations as they relate to the sex-role identities of both males and females. If there is differential identification with like-sex parents, we see the following in males:

(1) Fathers perceived as dominant in the family, the decision-maker with resources to solve problems.

(2) Fathers experienced as strong, powerful, and nurturant.

(3) Father sets the limits, which adds security to the child and helps him to set his own limits.

(4) *If* mother intrudes in some relationship with the father, if there is a power struggle she attempts to draw him to herself.

(5) When the father is absent, either physically or psychologically, it seems to indicate that boys (when deprived of a father from the age of two) tend to be less aggressive and less masculine and later may have trouble relating to males.

(6) One view holds that homosexual males nearly always come from these absent fathers and domineering mothers to which they have strong attachments, and that homosexual females often have weak, detached fathers and feel rejected by males.

Among females we find they may relate to either the mother or the father.

(1) If a girl identifies with a father who is both strong and nurturant, he would encourage femininity in the girl in contrast to his strength.

(2) If a girl identifies with her mother who may be dominant but not necessarily overly so if her father is also present.

(3) If a girl identifies with a masculine-preferred mother, she tends to be masculine.

(4) If she identifies with a feminine-preferred mother, she tends to be feminine.

(5) If the father intrudes in the relationship, he may make a "son" of the daughter, causing her to have difficulty with her identity as a female.

On the intellectual side, very definite intellectual changes, or ways of thinking, normally come about during the adolescent period. These changes are very important because without them a person cannot understand higher levels of morality. These changes are necessary but are not of themselves sufficient to produce the highest type of thinking. That is to say, they make it possible but do not guarantee it will happen. Piaget refers to this new cognitive change as the formal-operational. If we had one phrase to describe this stage between childhood and adulthood, intellectively, it would probably be "reversal of the real and possible." Up to this time the concrete, immediately available or real, has been primary and that which is not immediately seen has been secondary, or almost nonexistent in some. However, as we mature, the *possible* becomes the *primary*.

This involves several things:

(1) We can think beyond the present; can think abstractly and construct theories. A child is perceptive and descriptive while the adolescent is conceptive and explanatory.

(2) We can consider relativity; see things related to context. We don't take things absolutely as given, not word-bound. A child feels that all information is inherent in the data. This thinking relatively encompasses several changes:

(a) Now capable of hypothetical, deductive thinking
(b) Can think of alternatives; can hold one way constant in the mind while pursuing other alternatives. Can think in contrary-to-fact terms. This causes decision making to become more difficult since various alternatives can be seen. This forms the basis for establishing values and for reaching maturity at a higher level.

(c) Self-reflective thinking emerges. For the first time one is really able to stand back and look at oneself. This helps to observe self as seen by other people. This gives a newer and more complete sense of "I-ness." One is now aware of their own awareness.

(d) The development of time perspective. The person is no longer seeing just the present but understands the past which adds a new sense of continuity, of belonging, which increases the self-identity. In the present one can become more reflective and learn to inhibit some responses. The ability to look at the future gives a sense of destiny.

(e) Now the adolescent knows that names of objects are arbitrary and can be given in multiple ways and thus there is no rigid way of saying everything. This means they can now differentiate between assumptions and facts.

(f) Implications are understood. The adolescent can now understand an event in view of its context, contingencies, intentions, purpose, and motivation. Up to now he has judged everything on the surface, the obvious and concrete.

(3) Idealism. Now the adolescent can think idealistically. He can think in terms of general principles, not just in specific do's and don'ts. He can relate to affects, feelings, and emotions to principles. A person who can construct contrary-to-fact alternate possibilities in the future is an idealist. This leads to a kind of cognitive egocentricism or a knowledge of self as a whole with definite boundaries.

As the adolescent reaches this point in his journey toward maturity, he becomes more conscious of one of the greatest sources of ambivalence and problems for both the parent and the teenager. This is the problem of departure or the moving toward autonomy and self-law. It is the parents' task to alert their children so they can establish a disengaging strategy. This causes a lot of ambivalence on both sides. Some of this ambivalence is created in the way the adolescent goes about it. Sometimes the parents seem to send a double signal, for example, "Yes, I want you to go, but I will be sick with worry until you get back!" It is hard for the adolescent to distinguish between the real and the sham issues. The problem for both parents and adolescents is how to let go in a way that they will not feel abandoned or cause the other person to feel abandoned.

Parents face several problems in relation to this: (1) How much financial support shall they give and still lead the child toward financial independence. (2) A sense of lost mission—especially for parents who have built most of their lives around a personal investment in their children. They may feel that they are no longer needed when the children leave. (3) Fear of decline—departure of the children causes the parents to realize more completely their finiteness and that death is a real eventuality. (4) Some have guilt feelings or feelings of failure if all has not turned out as they dreamed. (5) Some parents feel rejected, cast aside. (6) Some have a fear of being out-of-date, no longer able to communicate with younger persons.

Adolescents also may have ambivalent feelings about finances. They usually want the financial help and the freedom from responsibility it brings, but they fear it means control. More sensitive children are afraid their parents or grandparents feel that is the only reason they care about them.

SEEING THEM THROUGH TO MATURITY

The adolescent also has ambivalent feelings about making decisions. He *thinks* he wants to make them, but when it comes to the part of accepting responsibility, he often tries to con his parents into making them. He also may doubt just where he stands developmentally and thus is afraid of accepting too much responsibility. He also knows that to accept responsibility (as in a profession) exposes him to the possibility of failure, which he fears.

Three ways in which parents often respond in these situations are detrimental to the development of the adolescent. (1) The first way is called *binding*. This may be affective binding, or trying to present the family as the source of all which the adolescent would be unwise to leave. Or it may be cognitive binding, in which parents may define or misdefine the motivations of the adolescent and at the same time deny all conflicts—refuse to admit that they exist. This disturbs the adolescent's self-identity and undermines autonomy. Another method of binding is the exploitation of loyalty. A certain loyalty is natural and the parent deserves and needs it, but it should never be used to make the adolescent feel guilty about leaving the nest.

(2) A second way of handling the situation is the *delegating* of a mission or living out an unrealized past desire through the child. In this case the adolescent feels unrecognized as a person in his own right and is forced, all the more, to his peer group.

(3) A third way some parents, unfortunately, use is *expelling*. The parent may see the child as a hindrance to a new career or marriage. In this case the adolescent is apt to feel unworthy and unloved. This tends to make him an untrusting person with no attachments. He proba-

bly would lack empathy and would tend to see people as objects to be manipulated, which is the beginning of a sociopathic personality.

Some factors that would facilitate autonomy are:

(1) Parental involvement (especially paternal) in the interests and problems of the adolescent. This interest should be obvious, but with a certain distancing.

(2) Affective intensity, but nonpossessing.

(3) Constructive family conflict. Such conflict strengthens autonomy and lessens the need to rebel.

(4) The nature of parental authority. The *locus* of authority—is it shared? The *grounds* or basis of authority—is it rational or is it blindly enforced? *Sanctions*—the way rules and regulations are enforced—are they consistent? do they accentuate the positive? Are they to vent the anger and save the face of the parent?

The whole purpose, as I mentioned earlier, is to shift the control from without to within. Where there is no self-regulation, there can be no autonomy.

Today, as I was thinking back over this long, gradual shift from infancy, dependence, and external control to maturity, independence, and internal control, I thought of all the hopes and dreams and prayers that go into the process. I remembered a poem of Victor Hugo that I learned long ago:

> Be like the bird, who
> Halting in his flight
> On a limb too slight
> Feels it give way beneath him
> Yet sings,
> Knowing he hath wings.

That's it! I said to myself. We want to help give children a deep consciousness of what they are and all they were meant to be. A consciousness so deep and satisfying that no misfortunes or "limbs too slight" will take it from them.

That will, indeed, take all of us!

Notes

CHAPTER 4

1. Benjamin Bloom, *Stability and Change in Human Characteristics* (New York: John Wiley, 1964).
2. *Crisis in Child Mental Health: Challenge for the 1970's*, A Report of the Joint Commission on Mental Health of Children (New York: Harper and Row, 1969), p. 313.

CHAPTER 6

1. Maya Pine, "The Superkids," *Psychology Today*, Vol. 12, No. 8, 12 January 1979, p. 61 f.
2. Ibid., p. 61.
3. Michael Rutter, "Early Sources of Security and Competency," *Human Growth and Development*, Jerome Brunner and Alison Garton, ed. (Oxford: Oxford University Press, 1978).

CHAPTER 8

1. Robert J. Havighurst, *Developmental Tasks and Education*, Second Edition (New York: Longmans, Green, and Co., 1952).
2. Helen Parkhurst, *Exploring the Child's World* (New York: Appleton-Century-Crofts, 1951), pp. 256-268.

CHAPTER 9

1. Robbie Trent, *Your Child and God* (New York: Harper and Row, 1952), p. 27.
2. Ibid., pp. 1-12.